Color test page

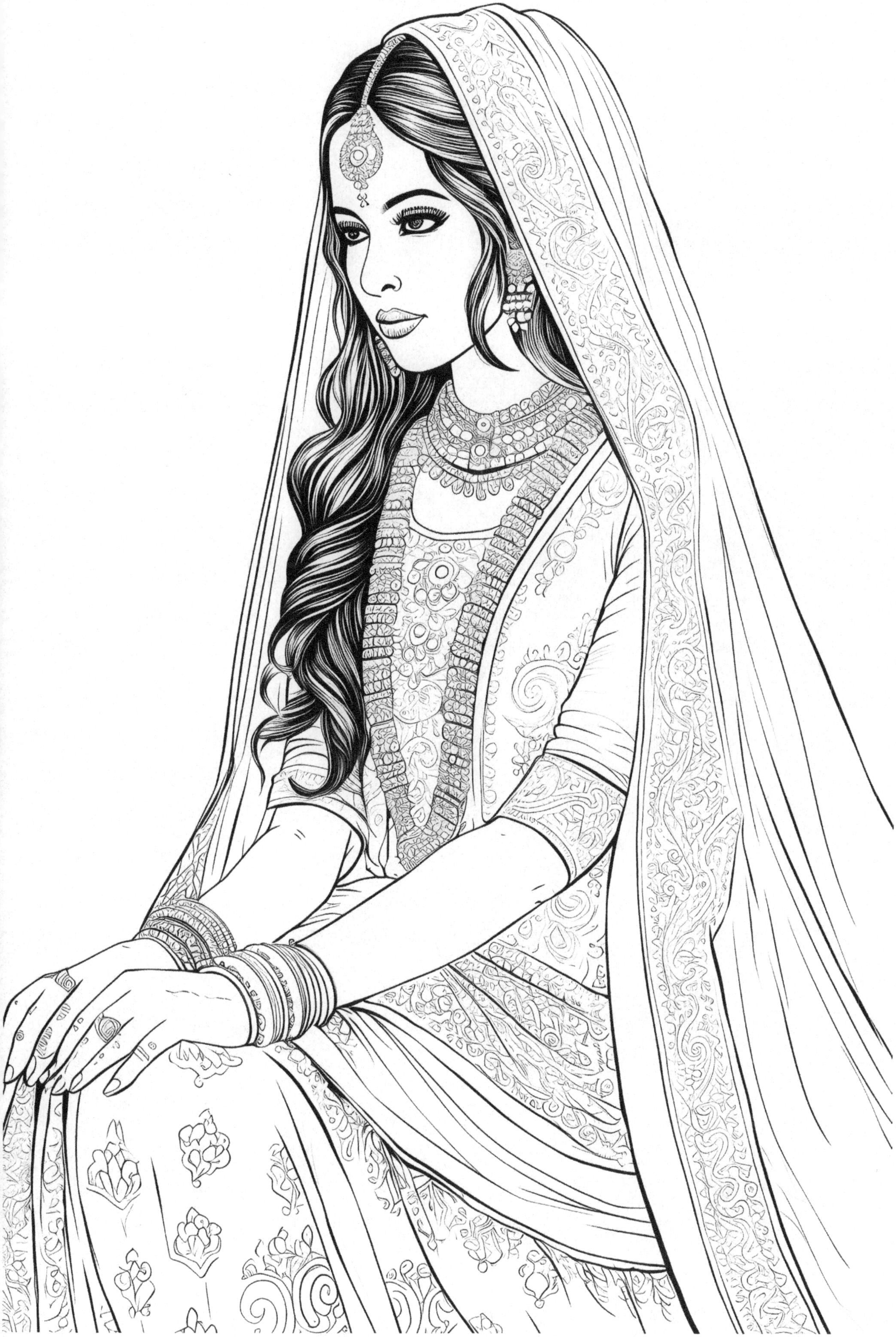

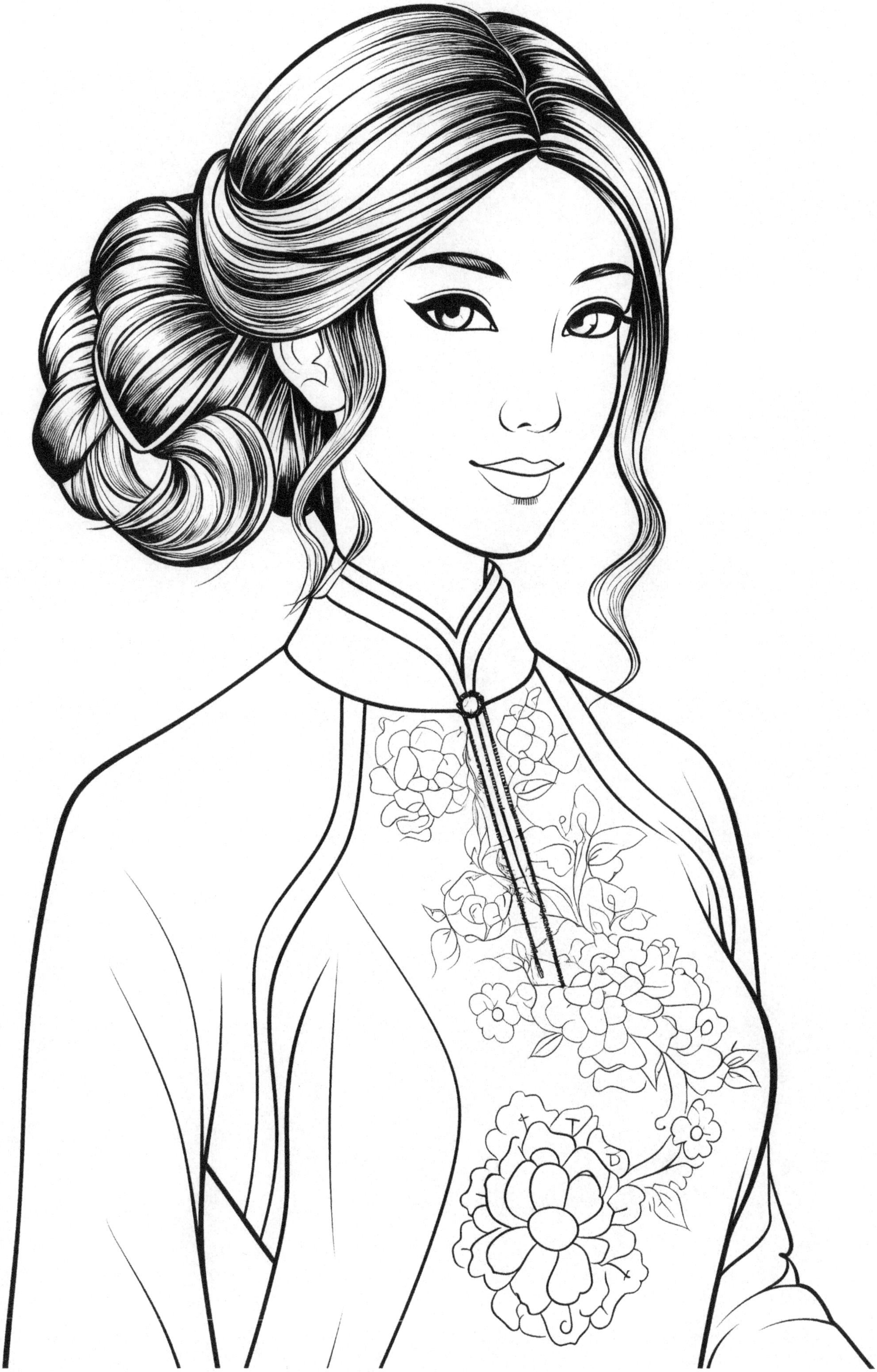

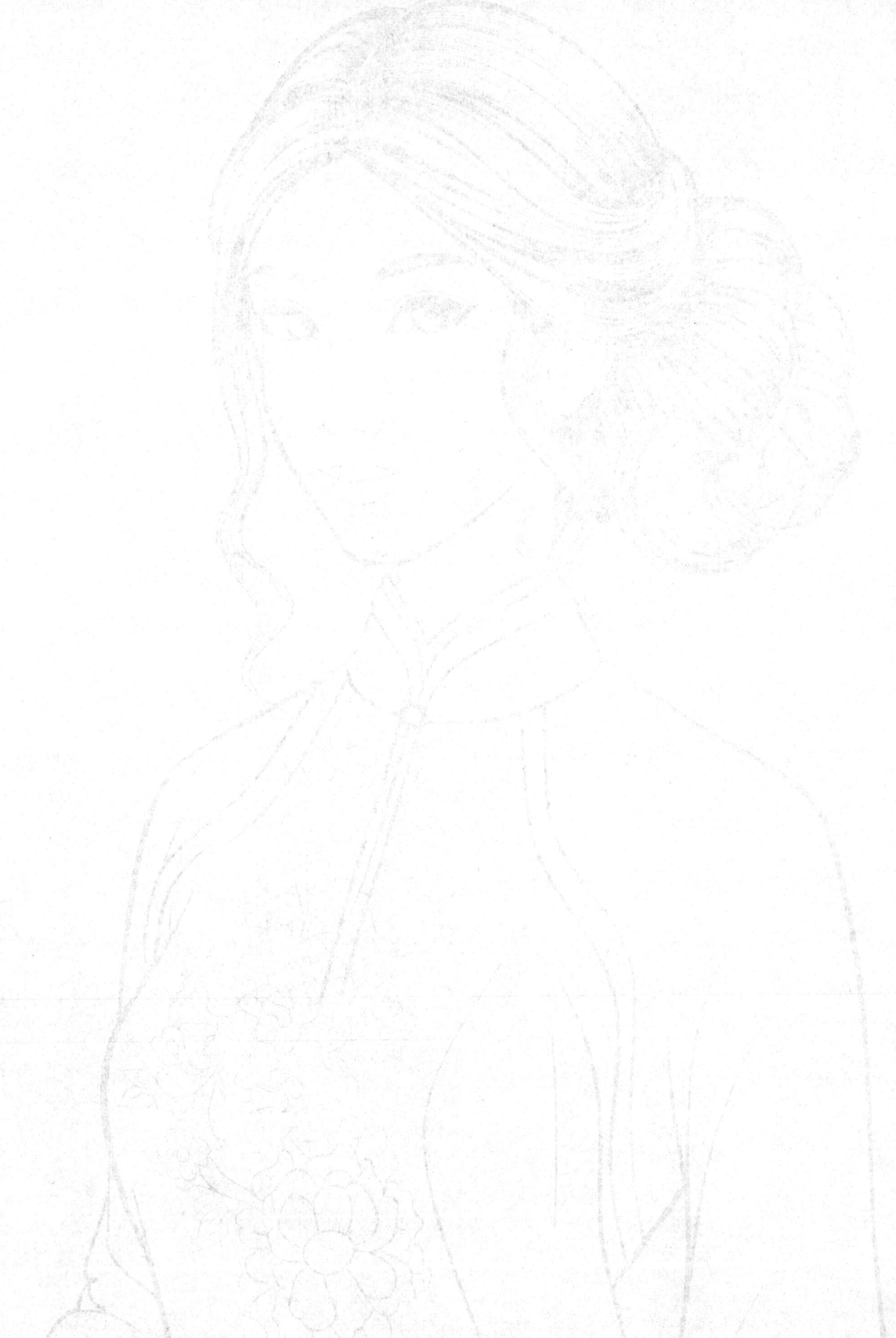

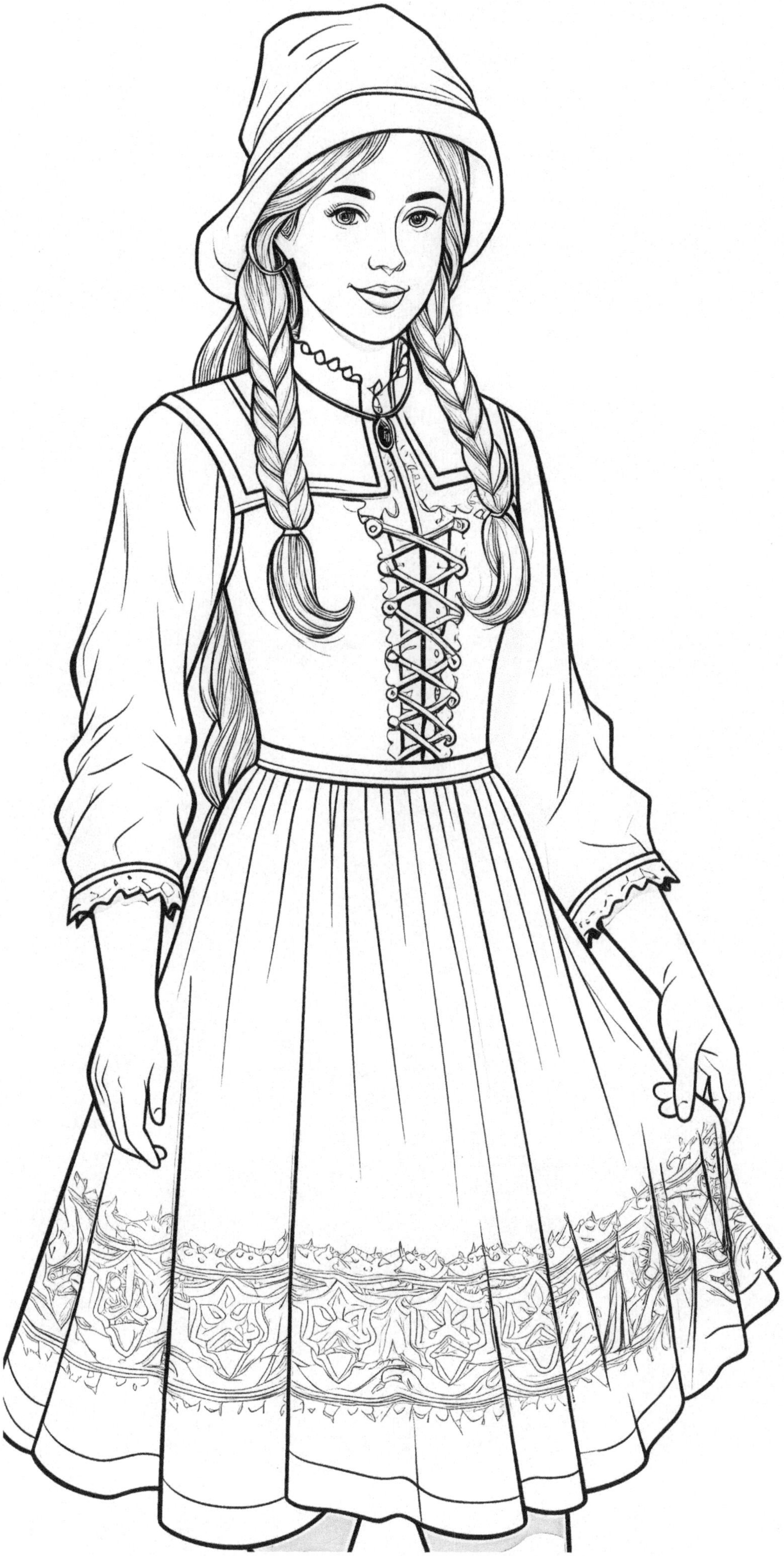

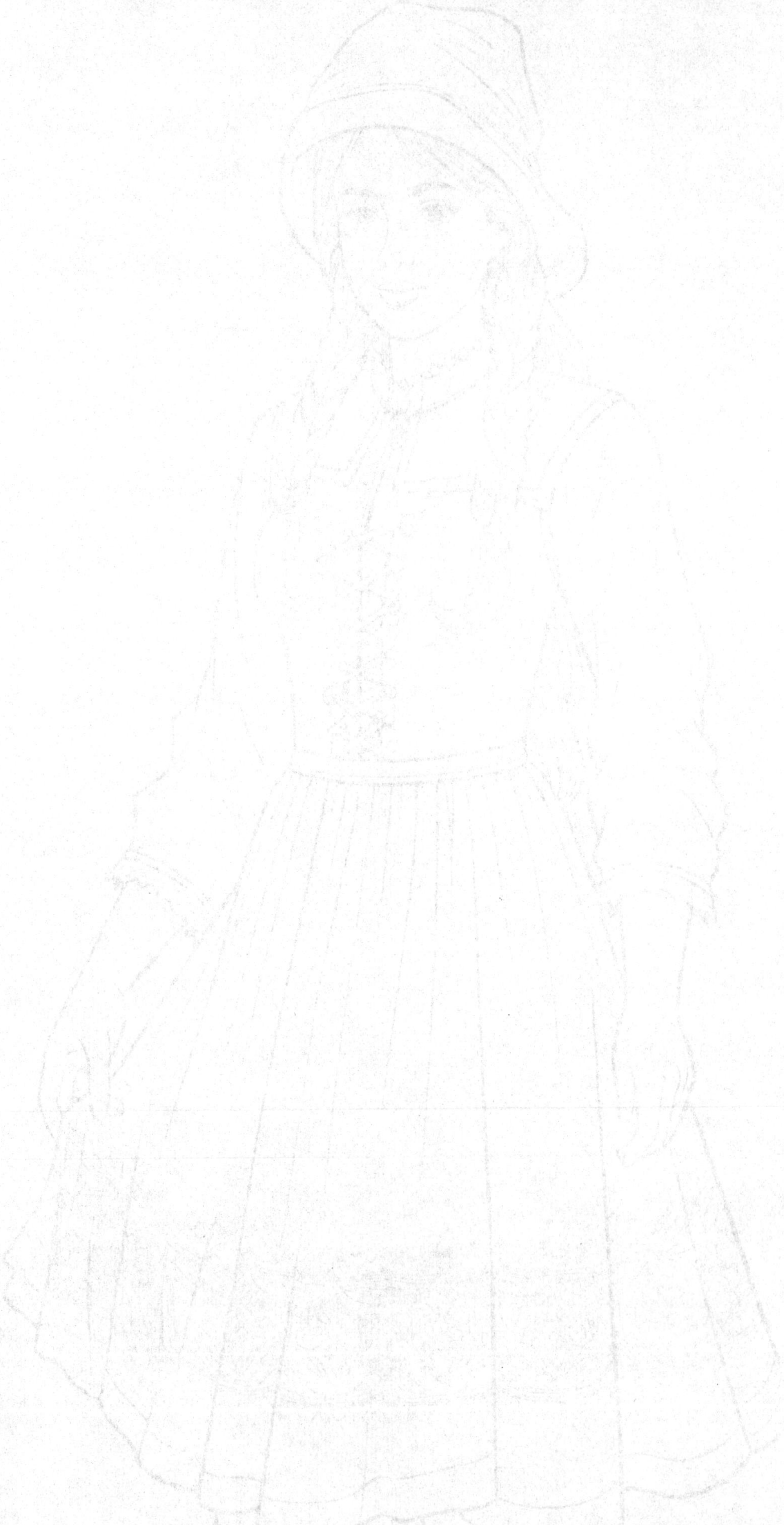

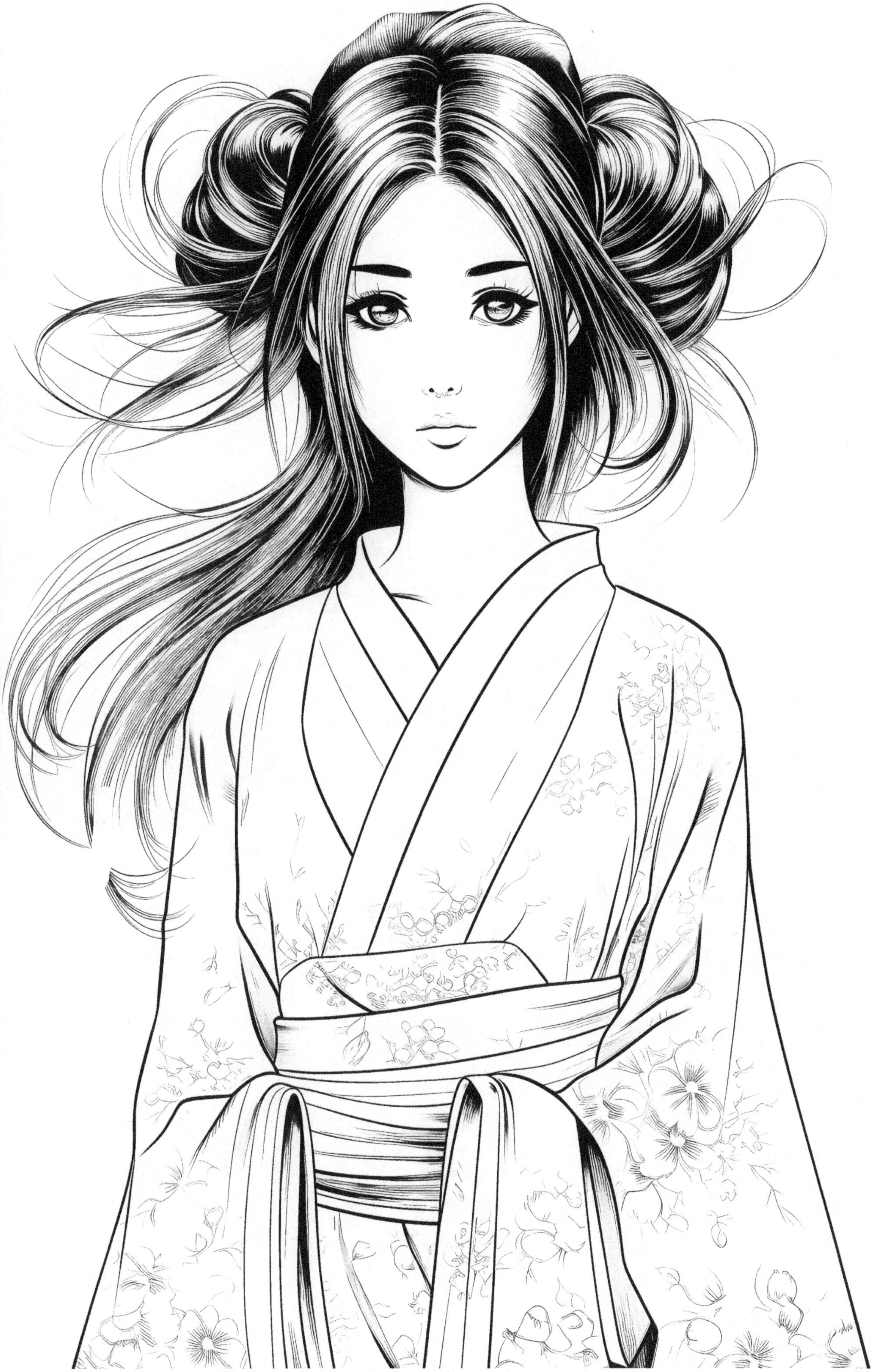

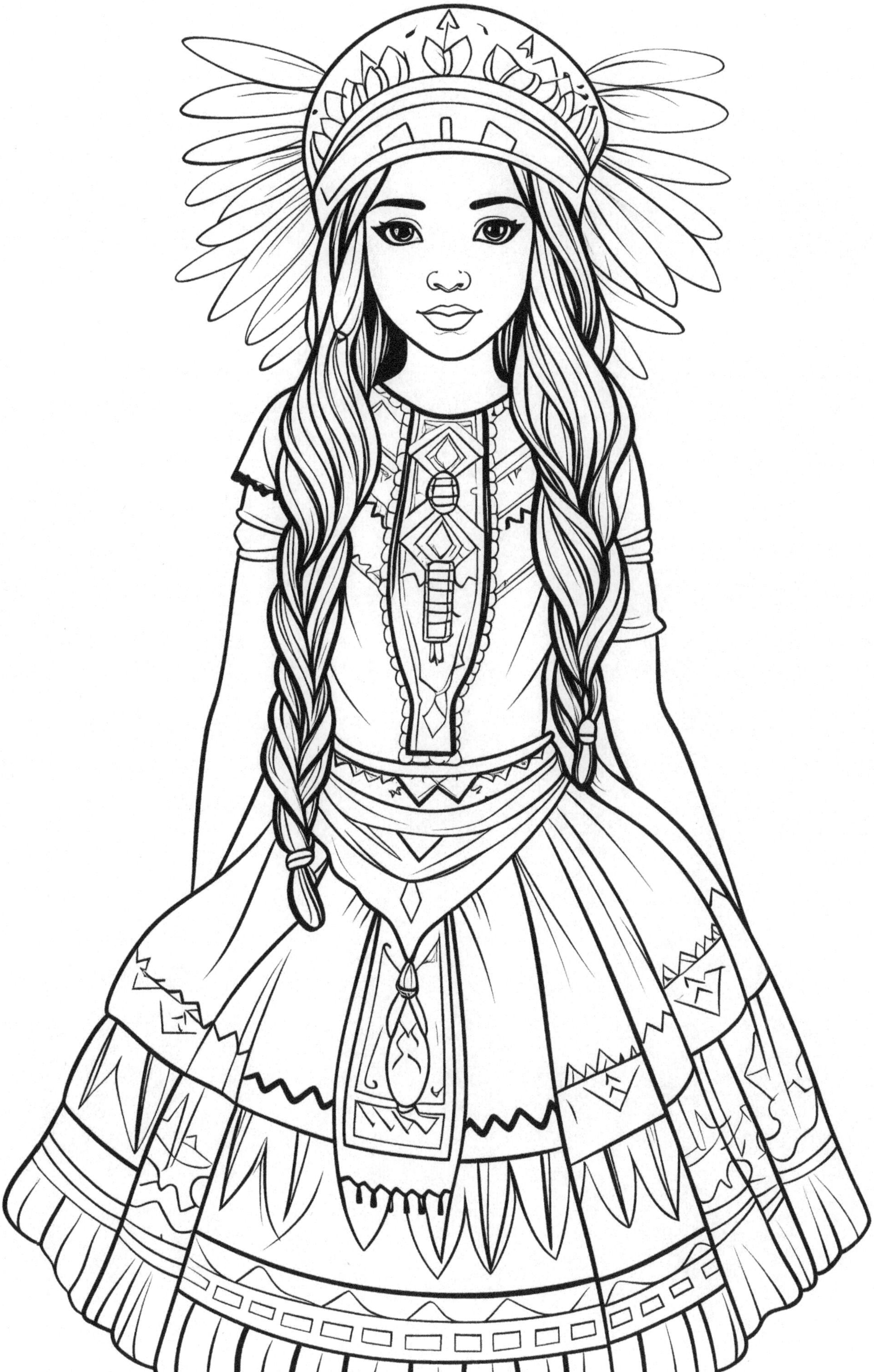

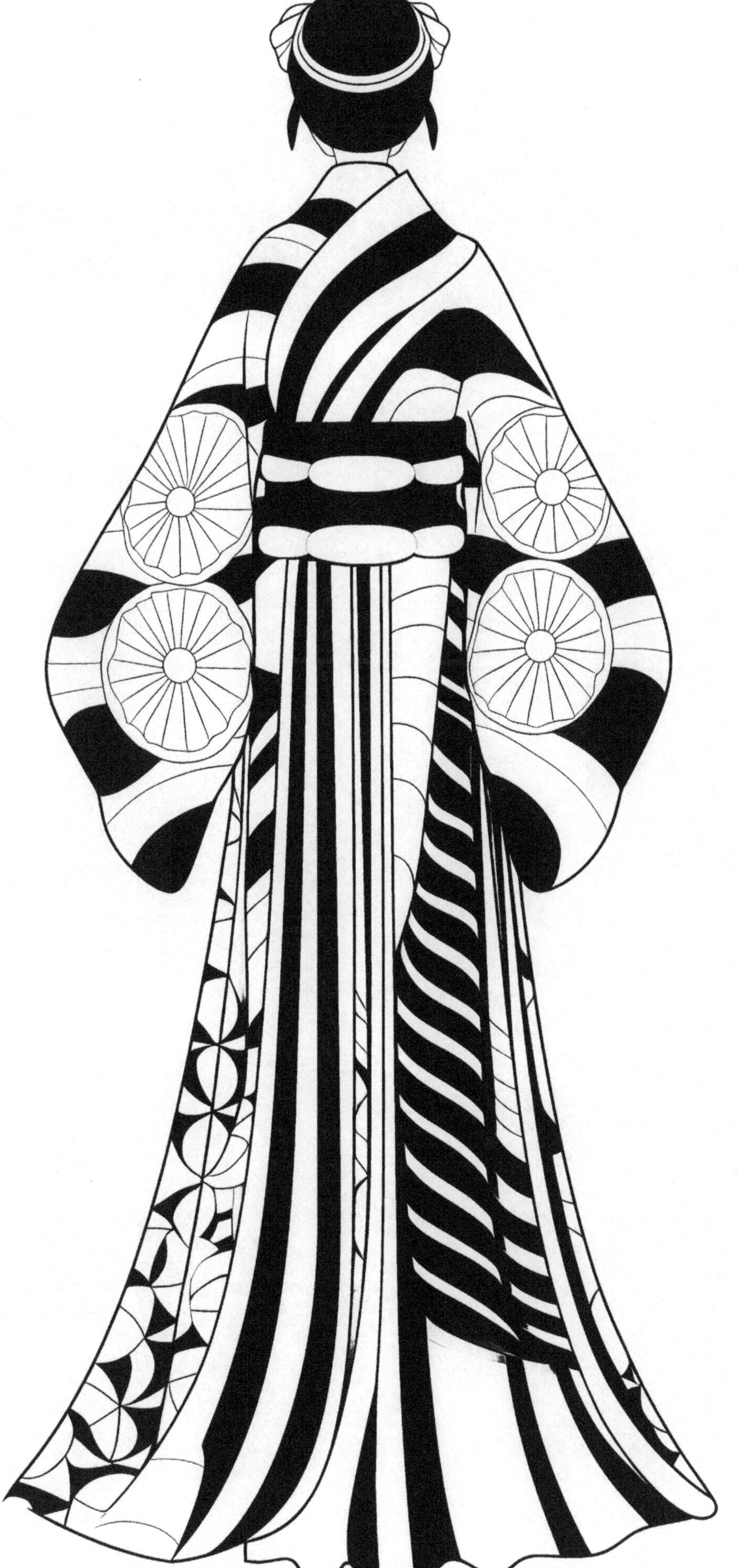

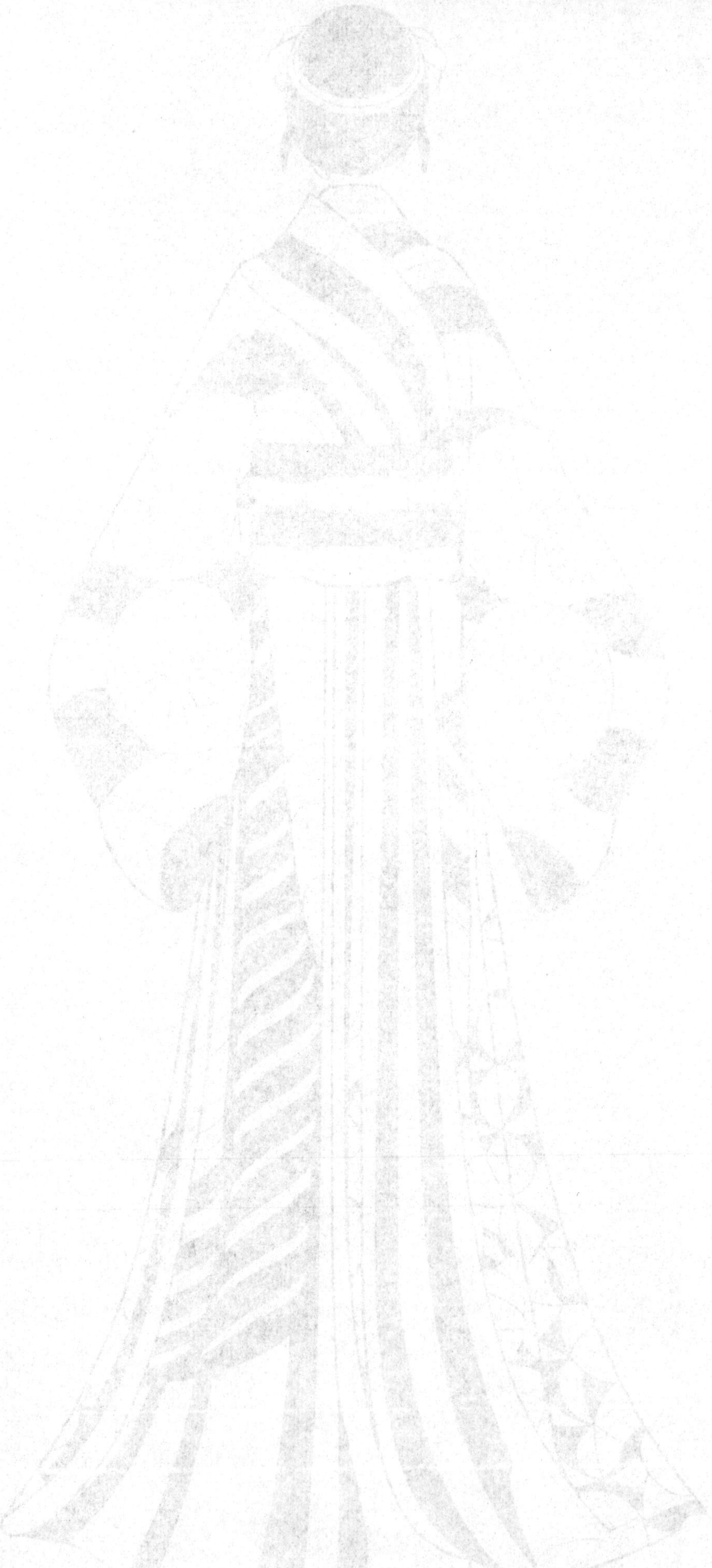

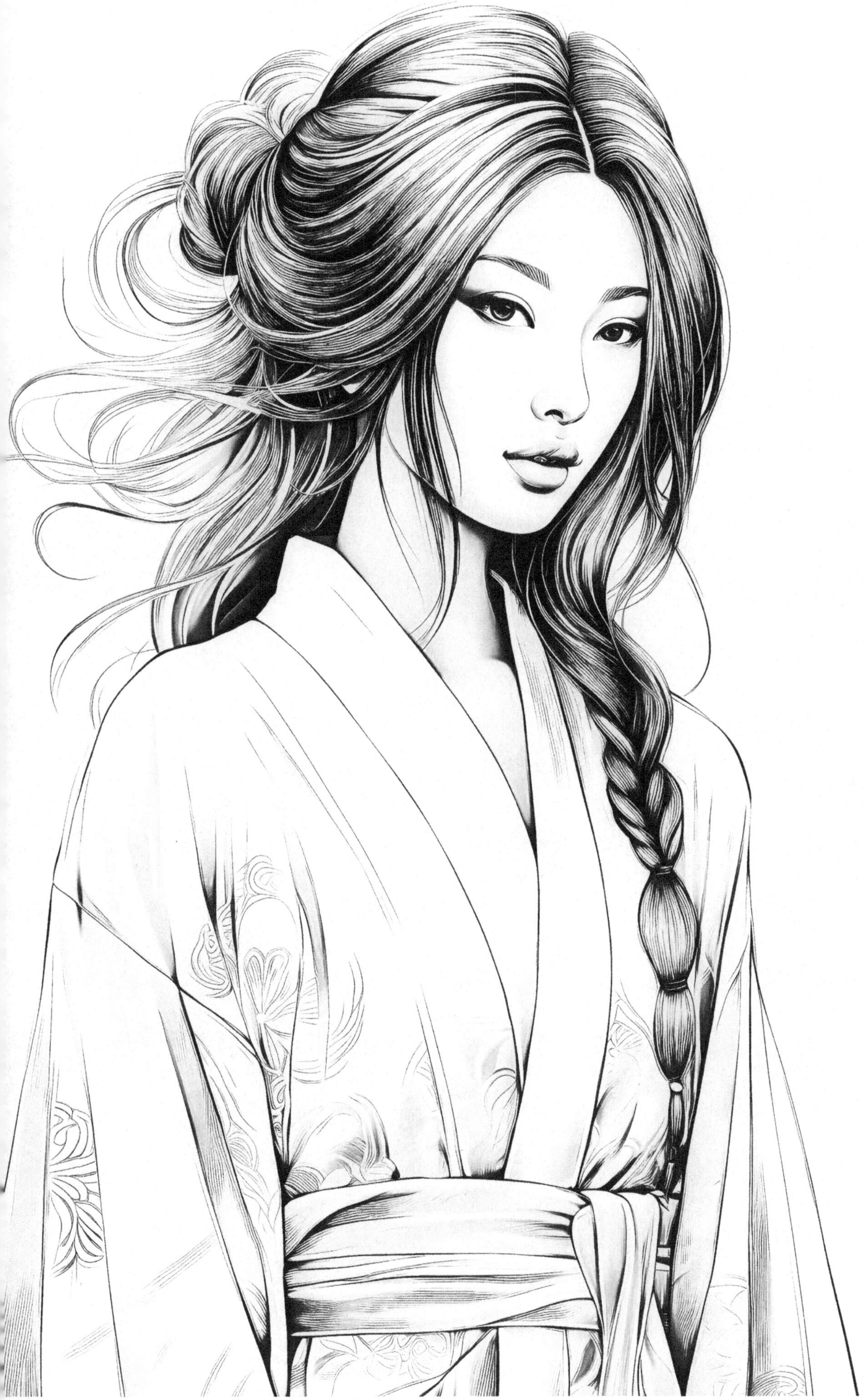

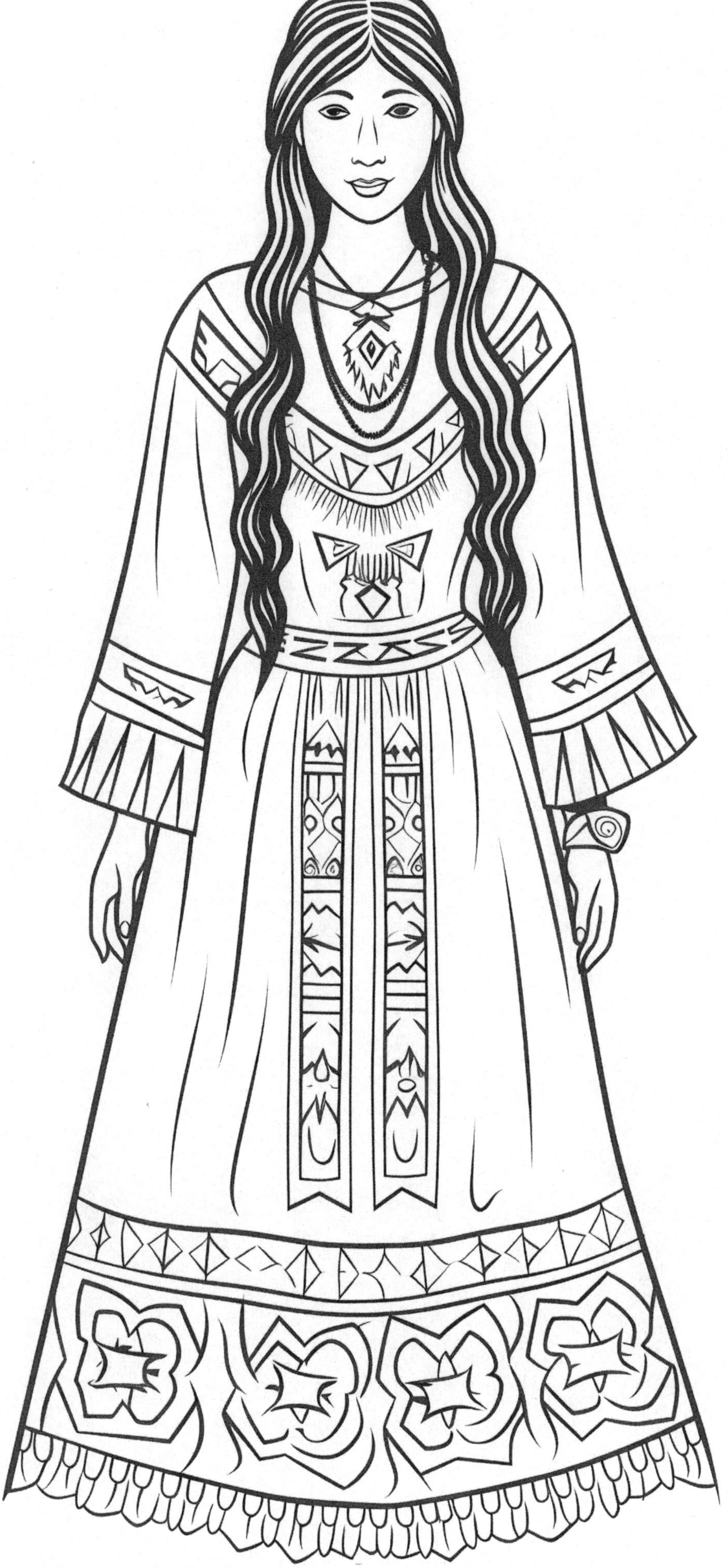

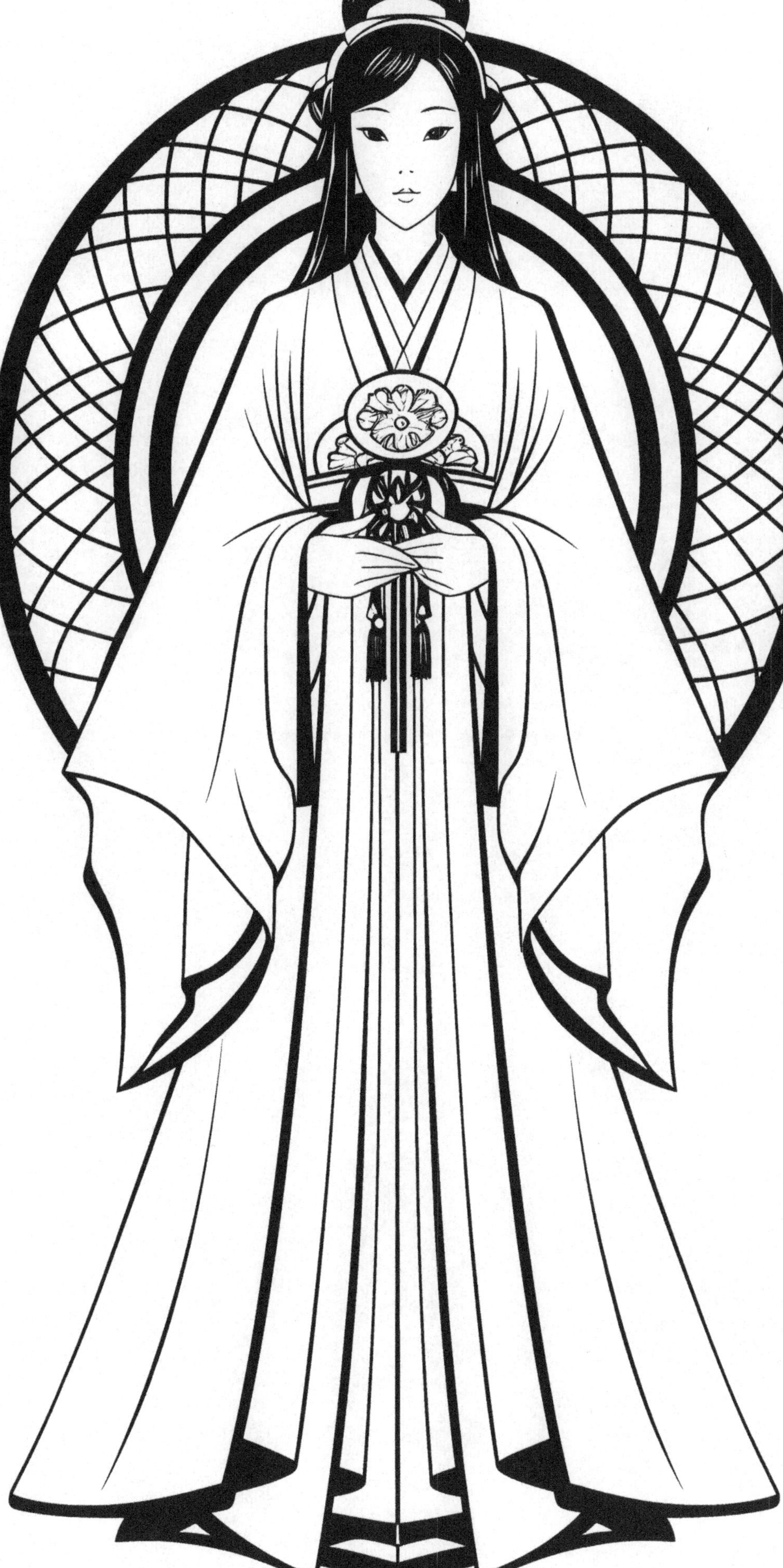

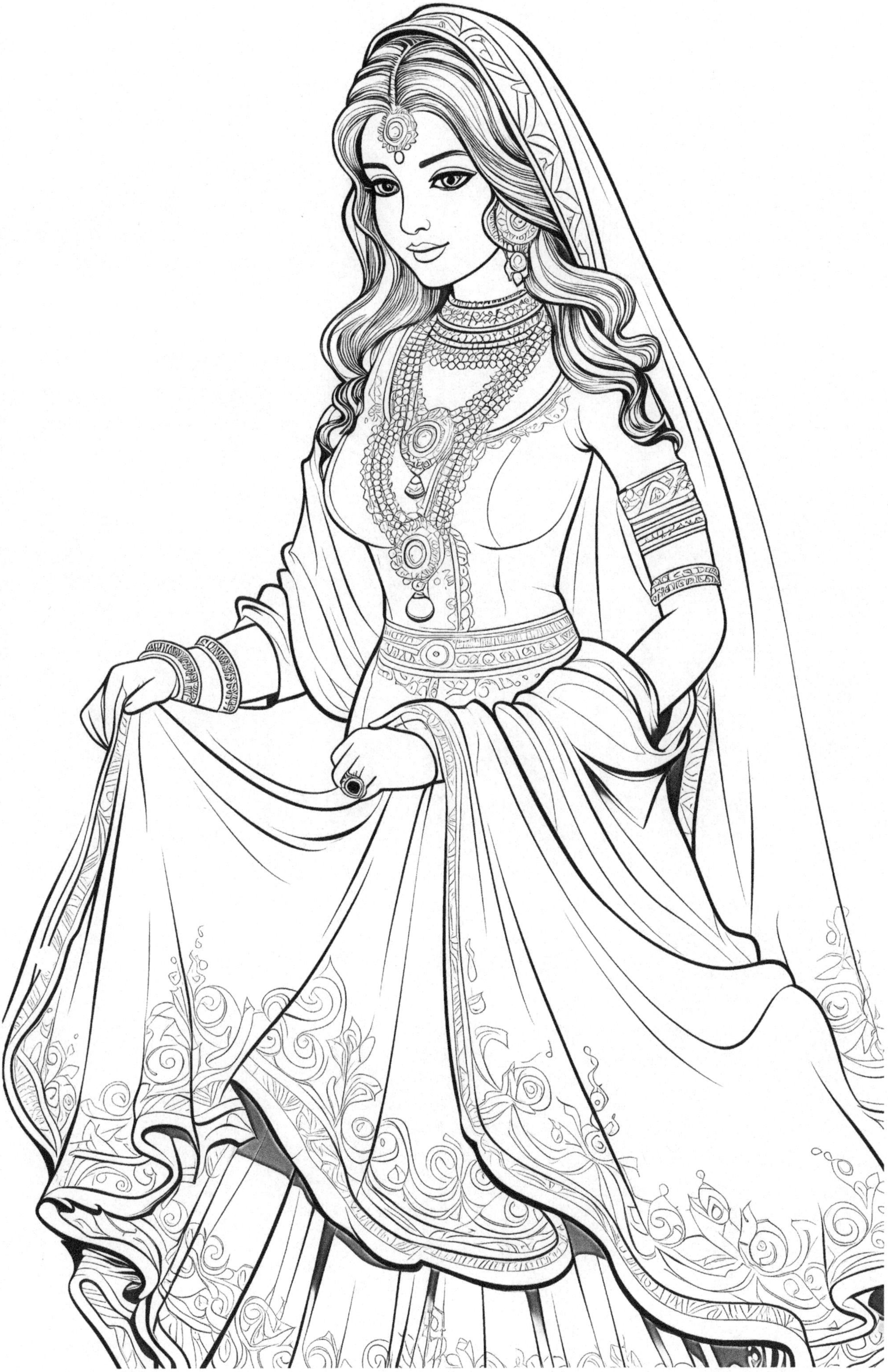

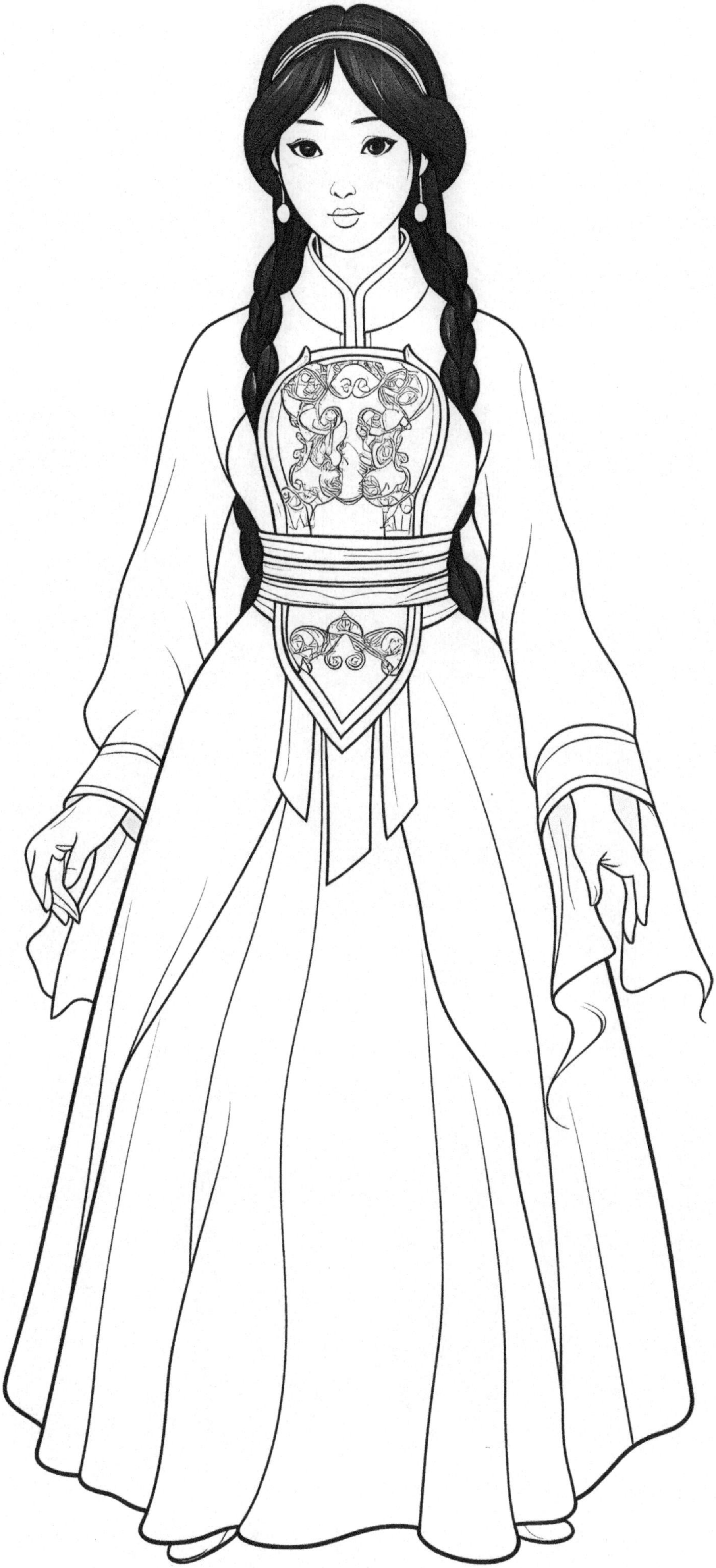

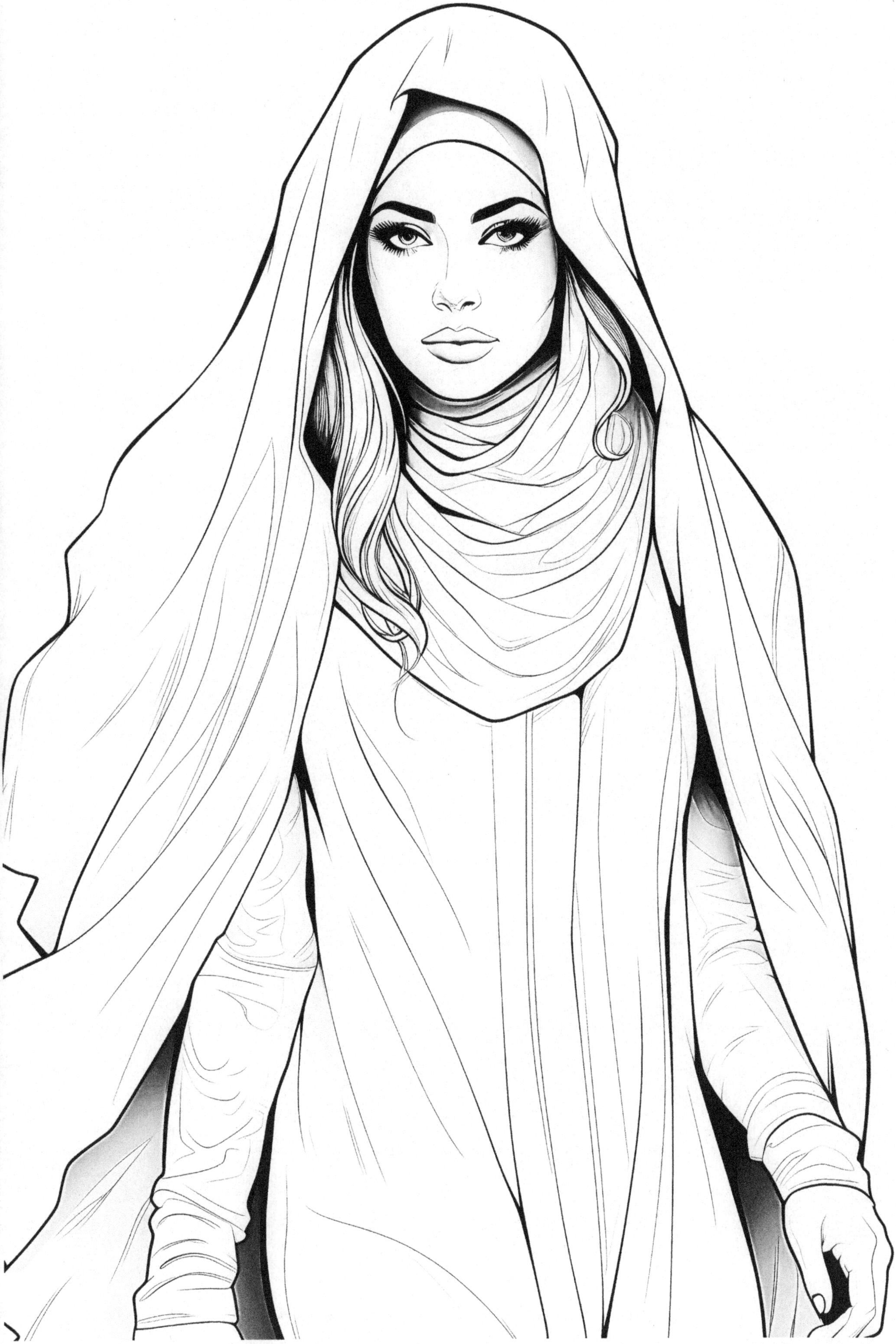

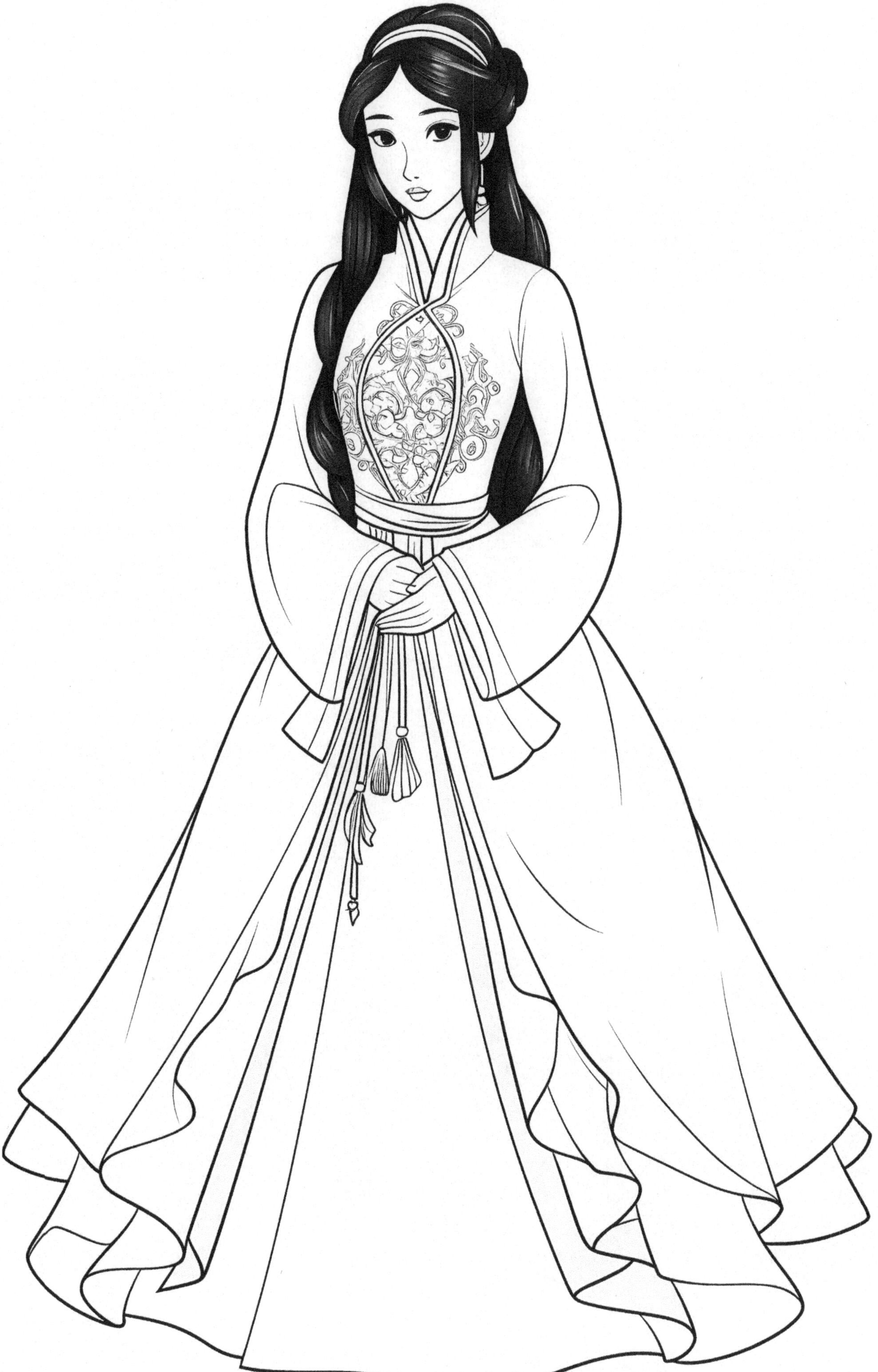

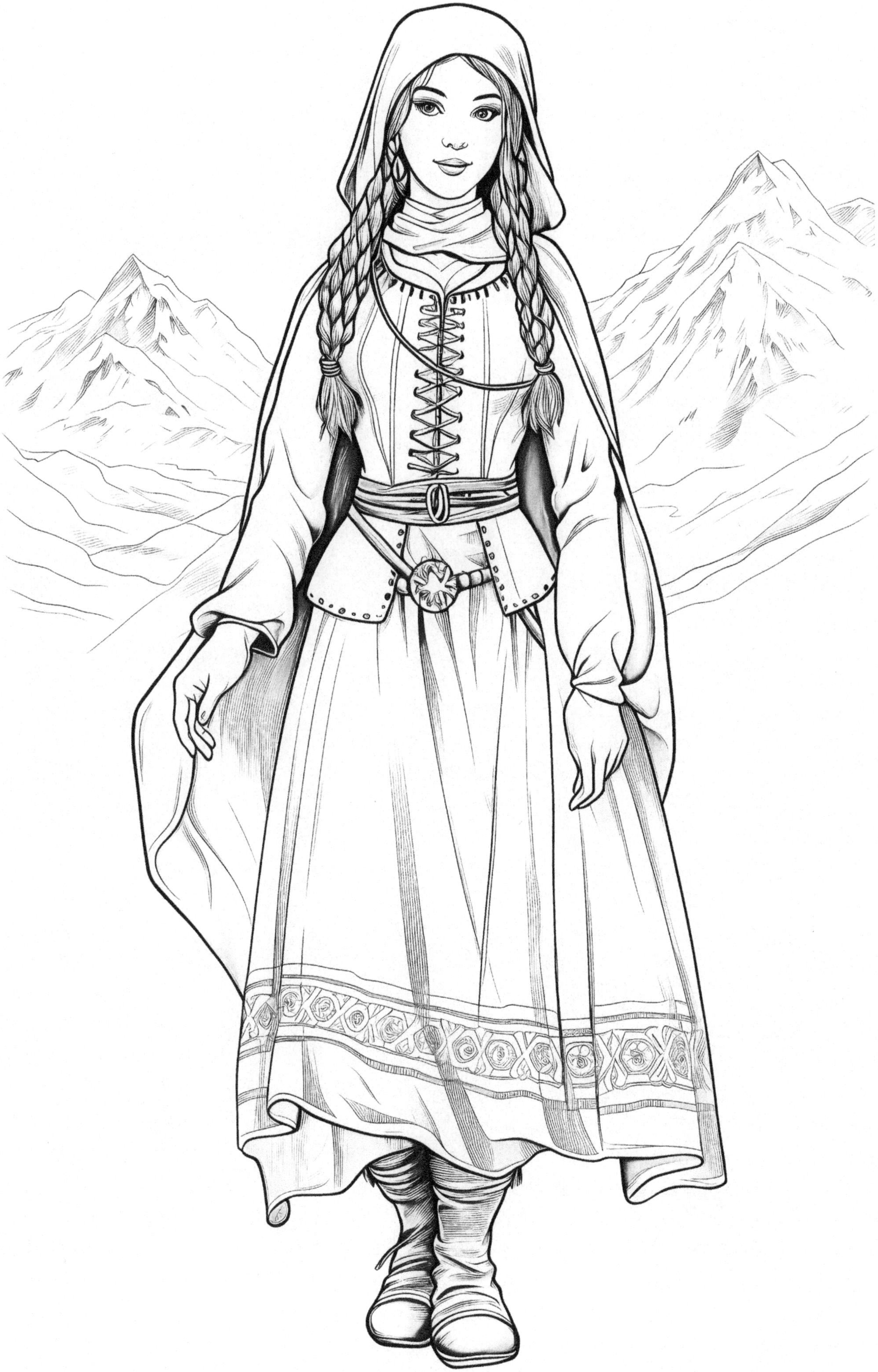

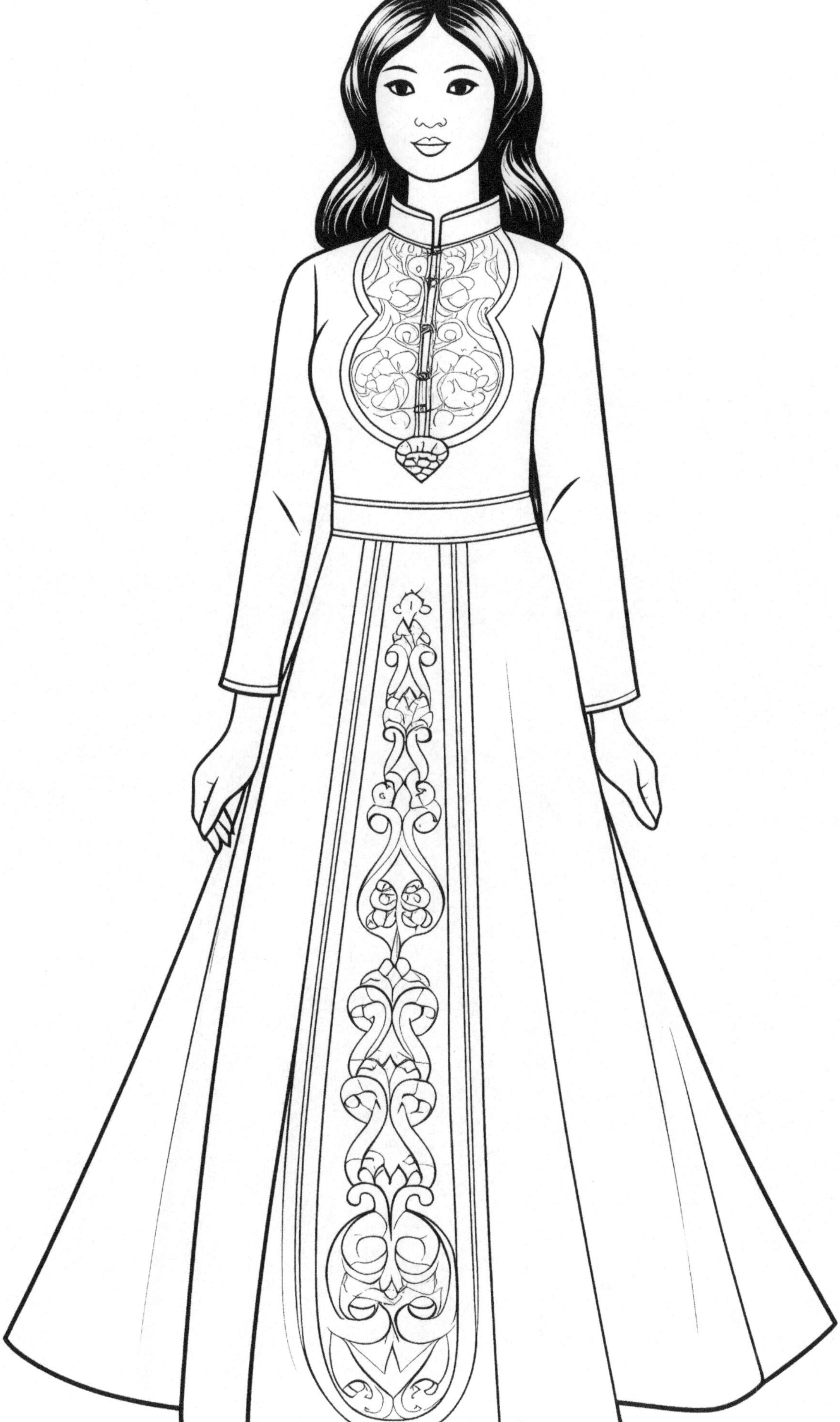

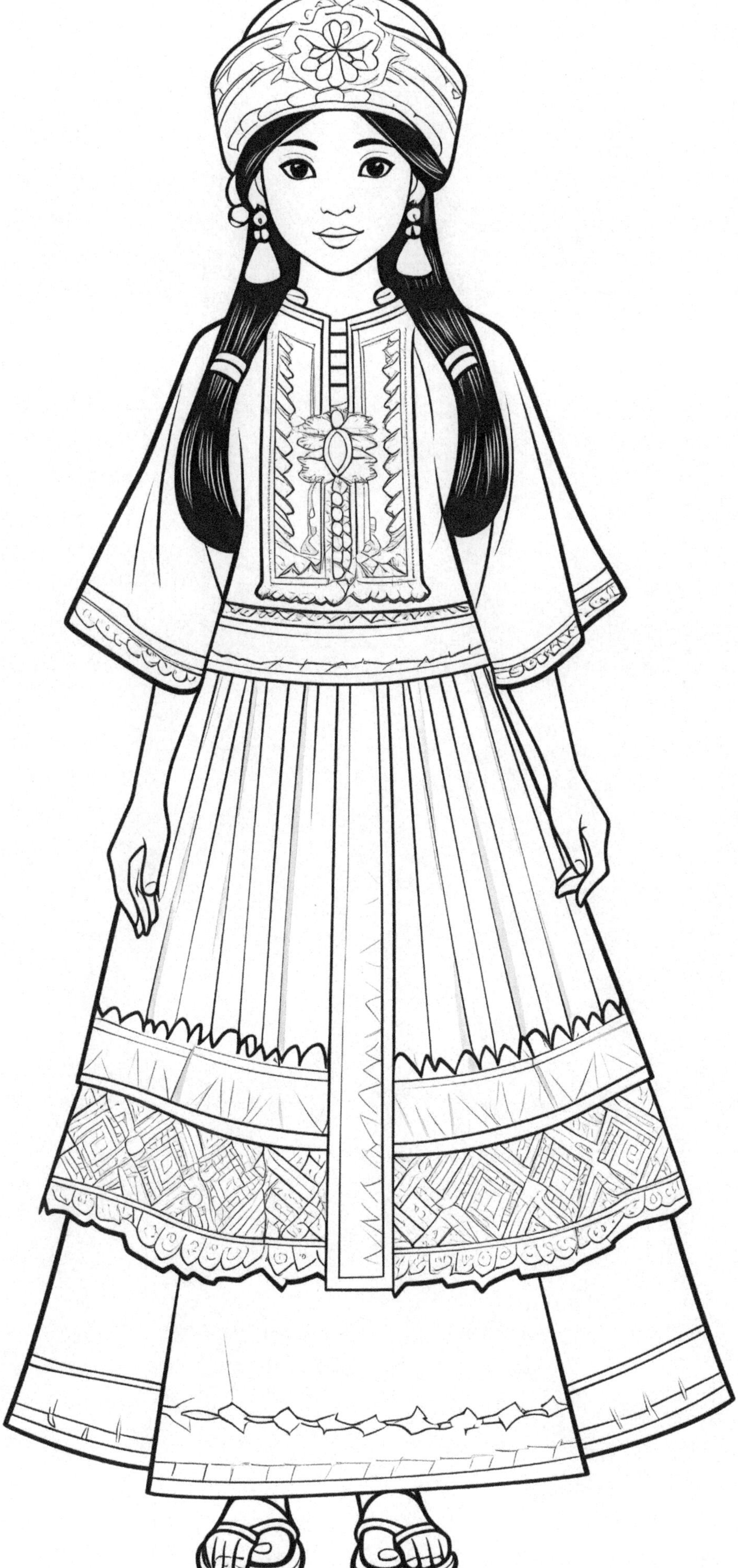

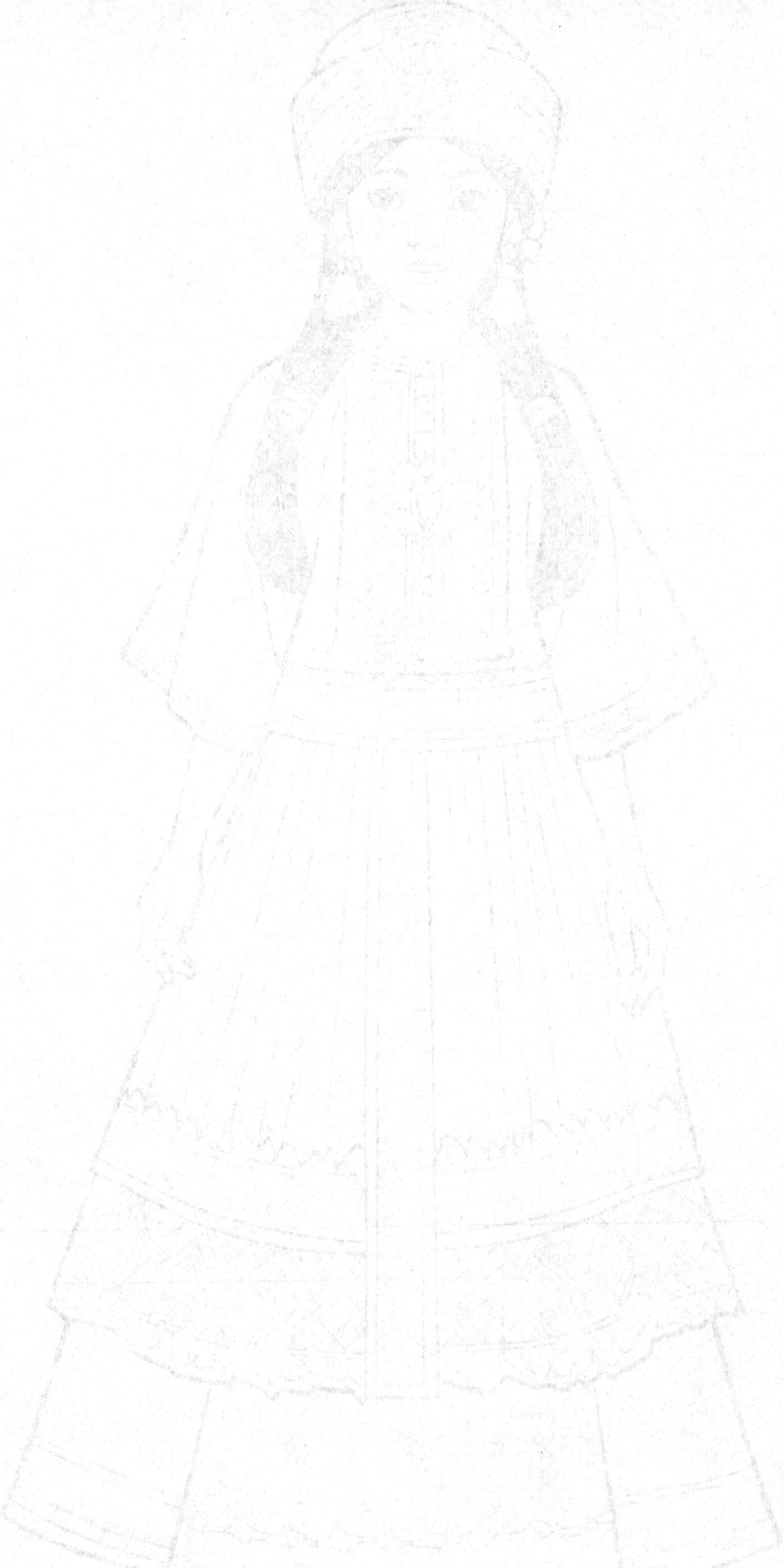

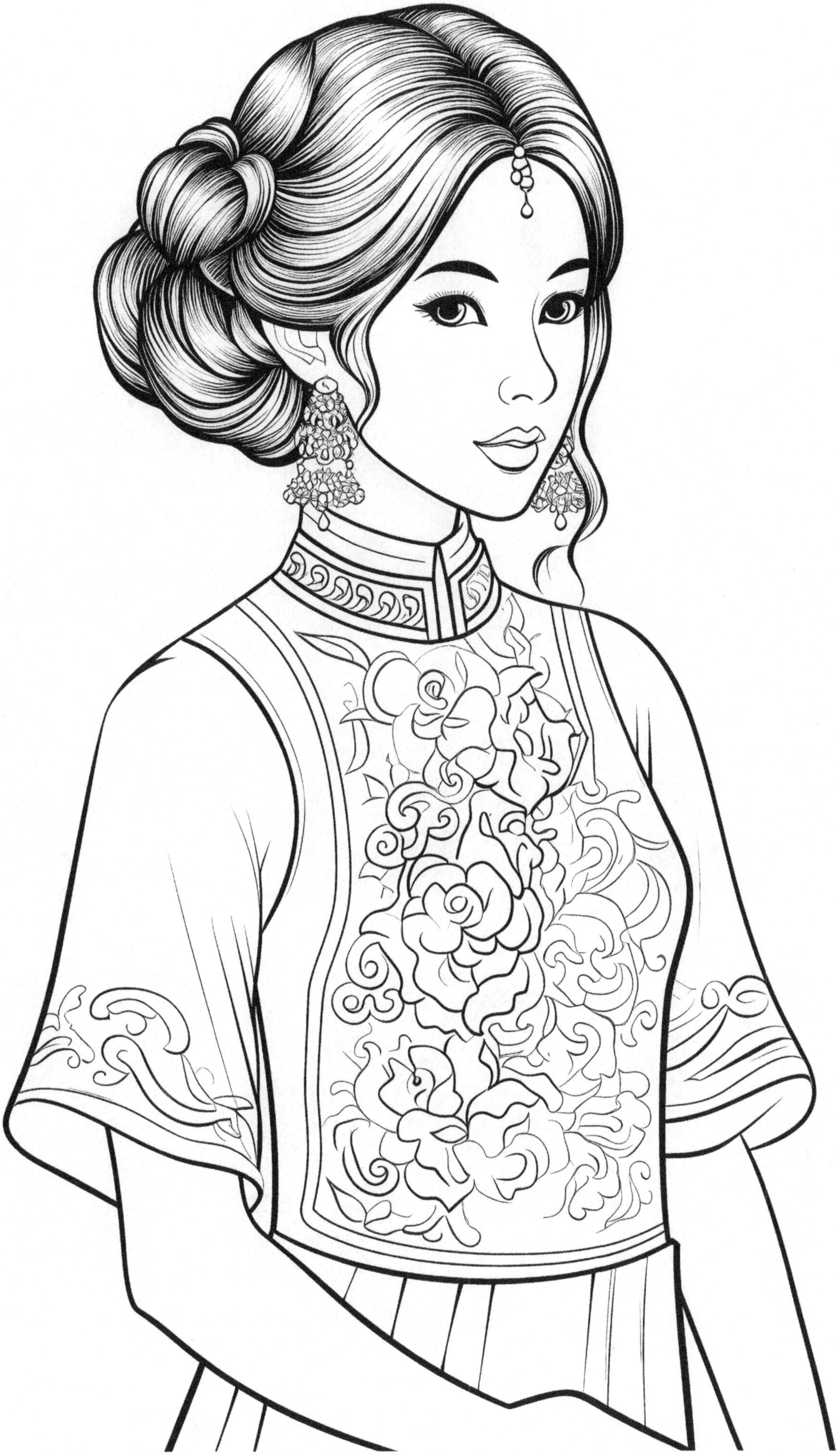

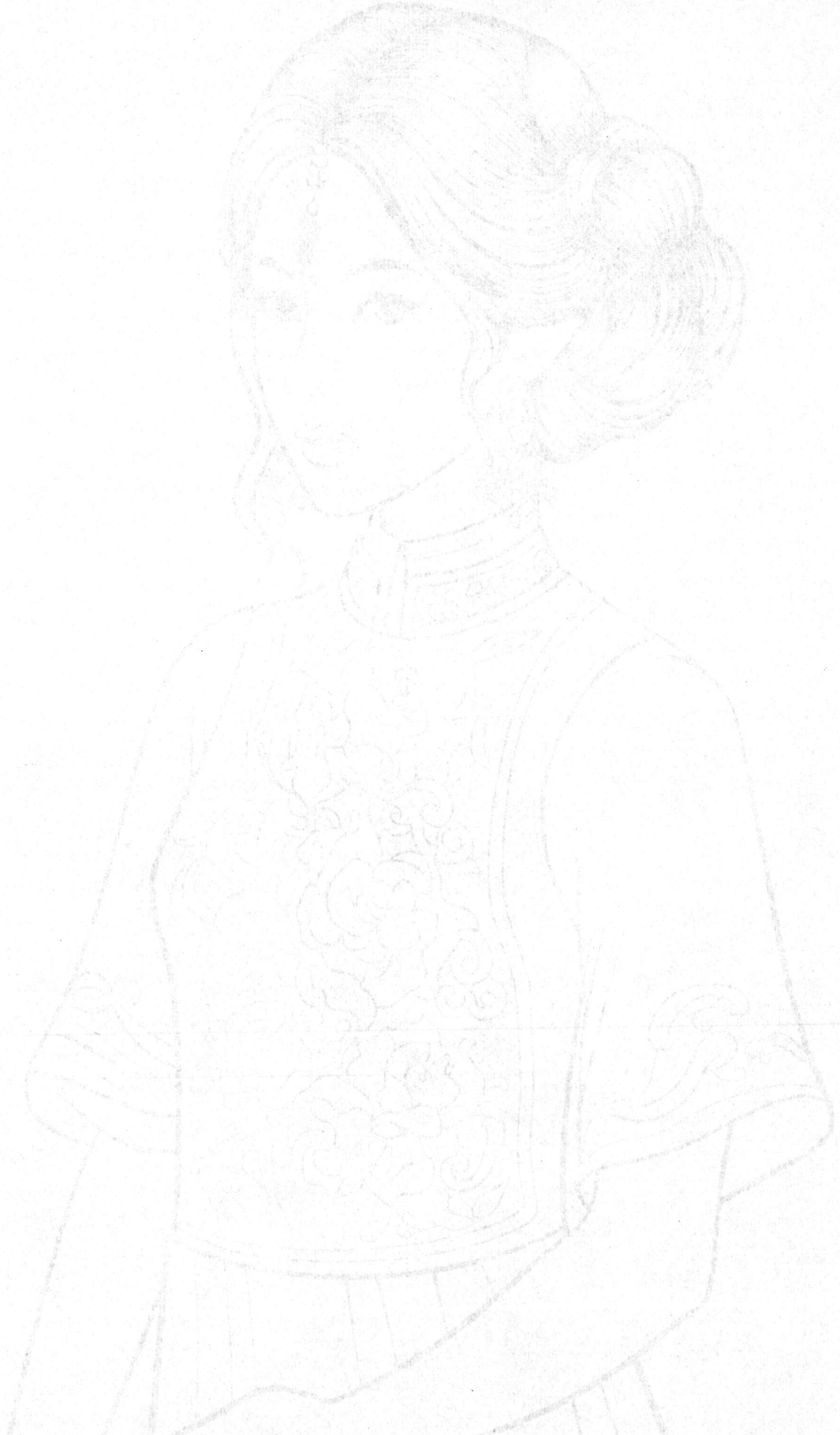

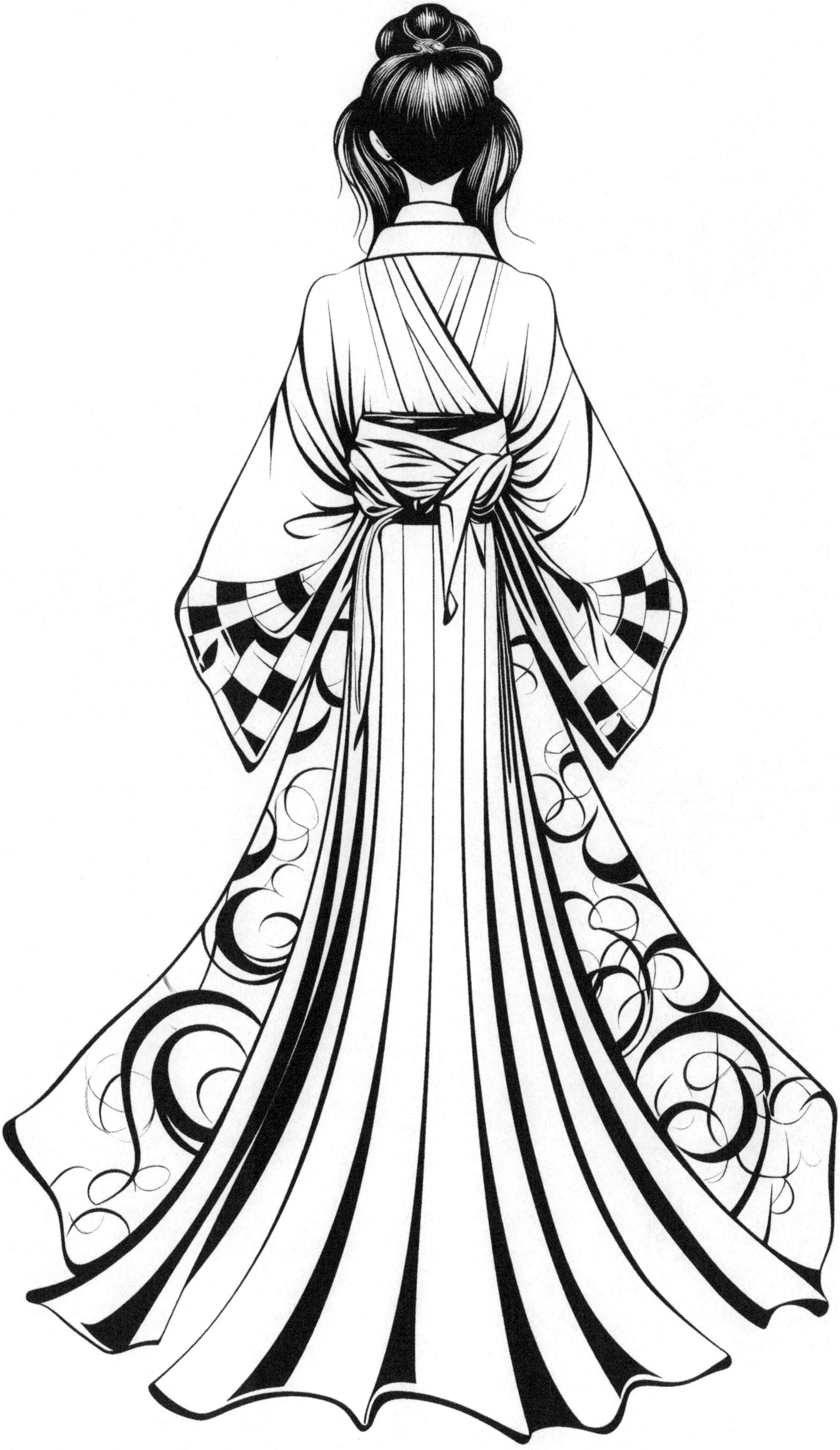

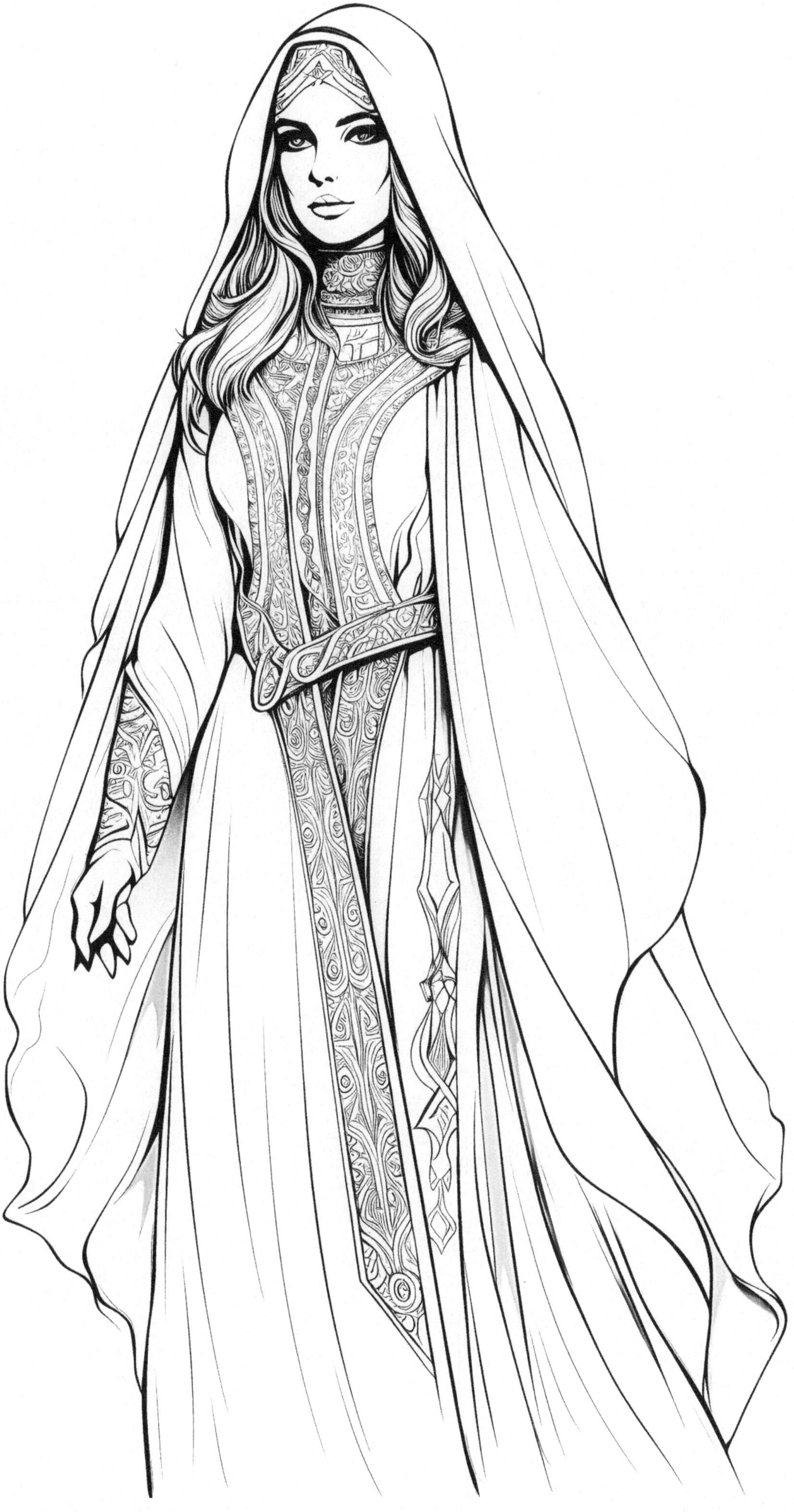

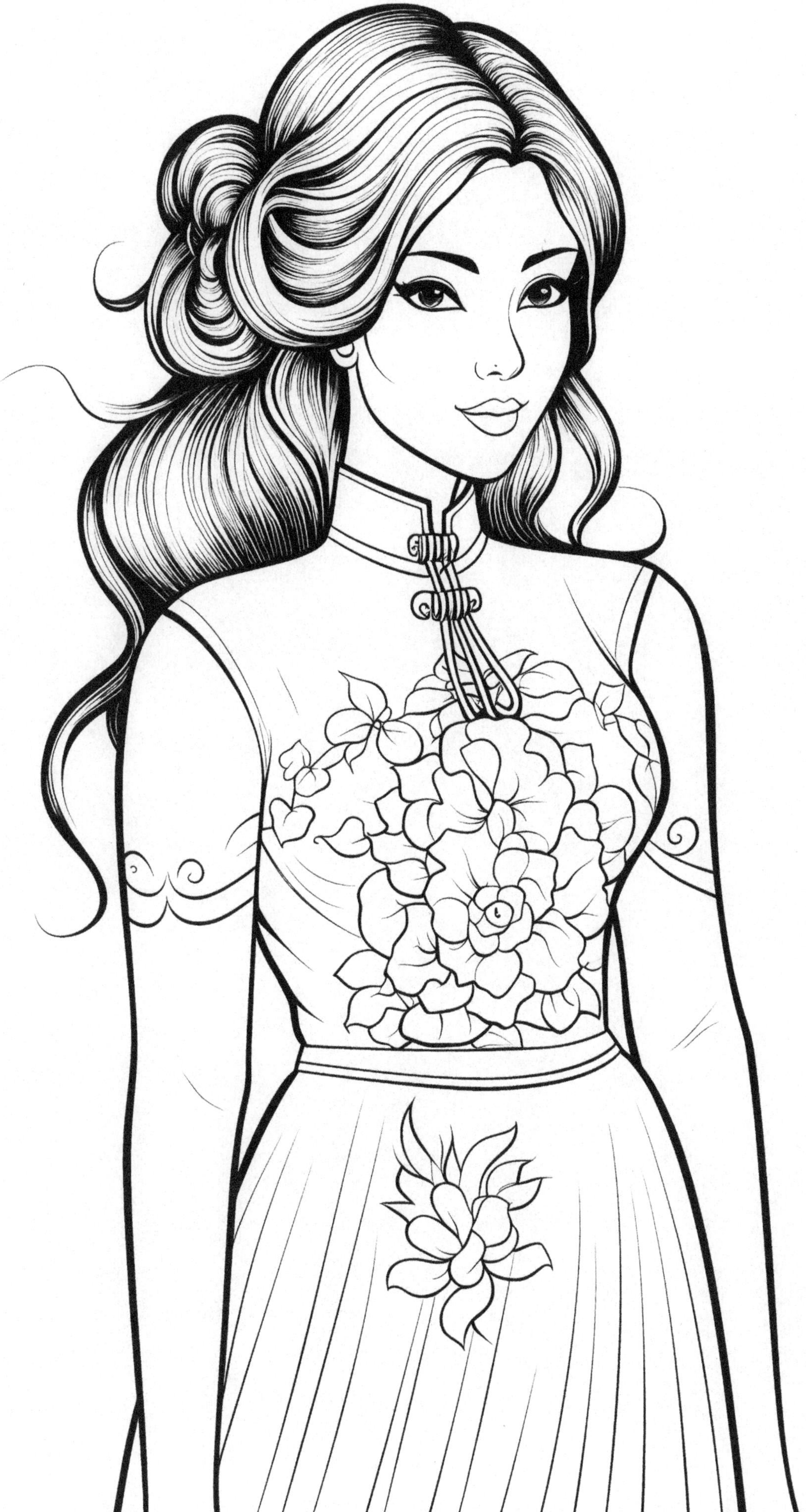

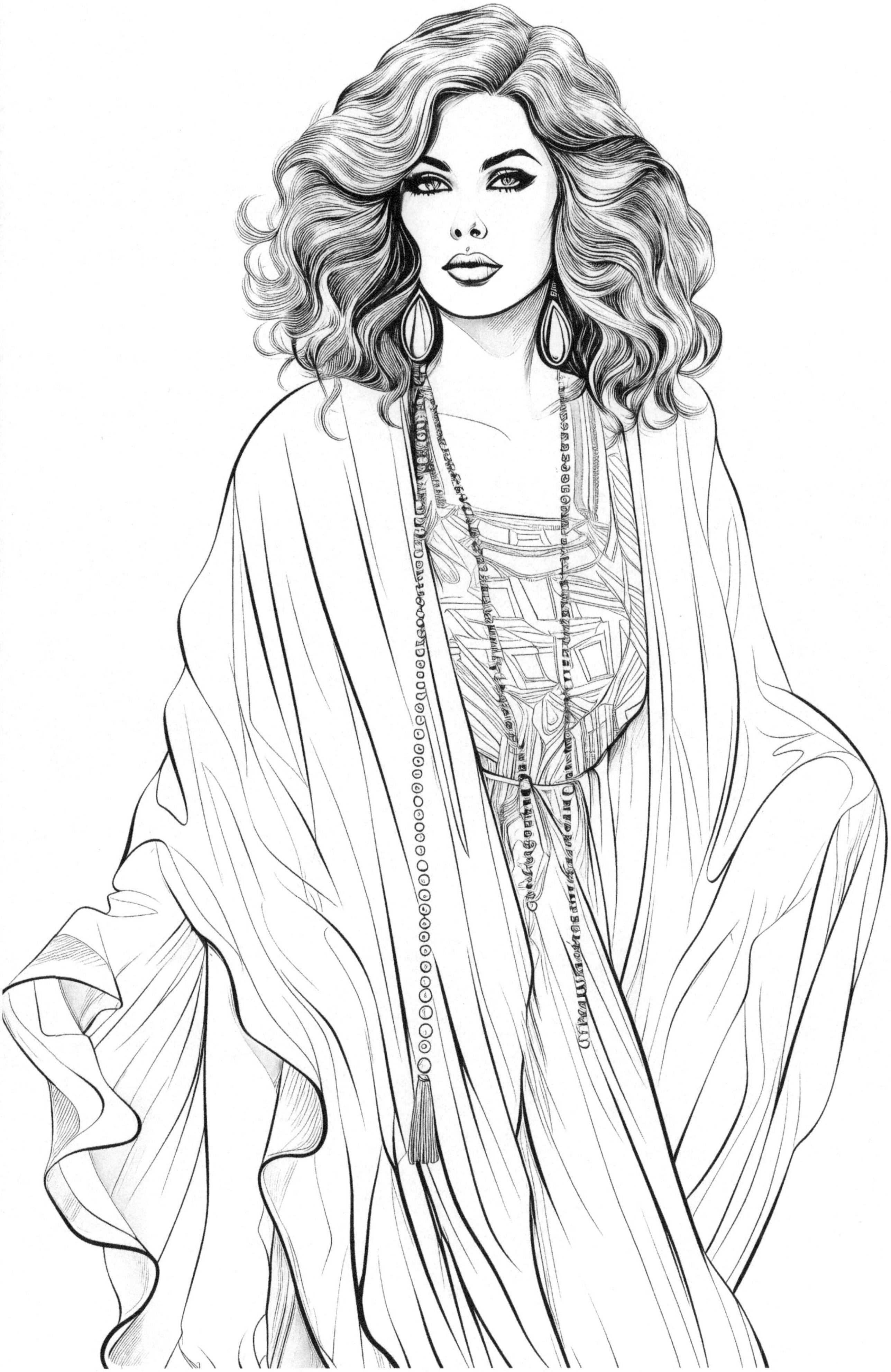

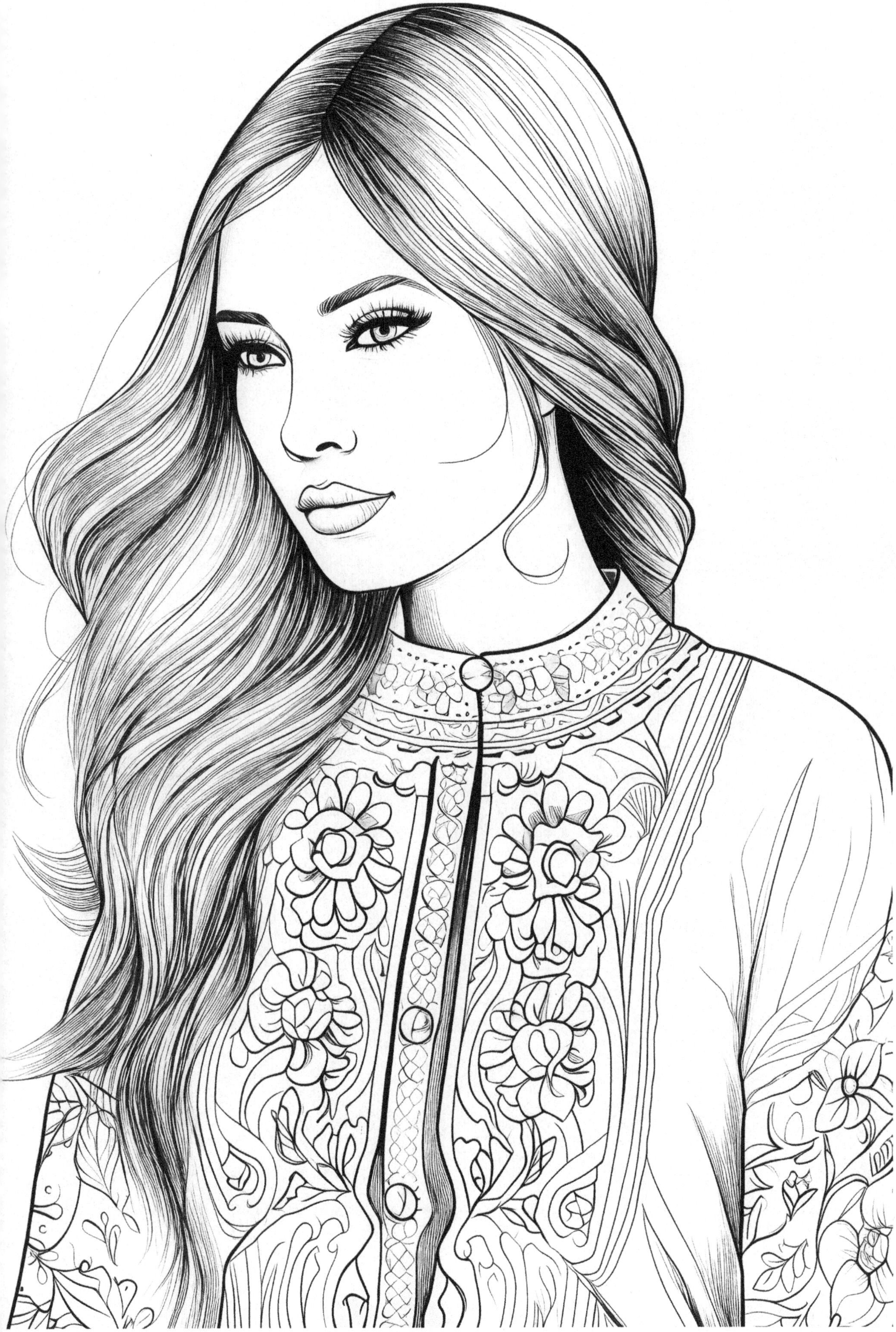

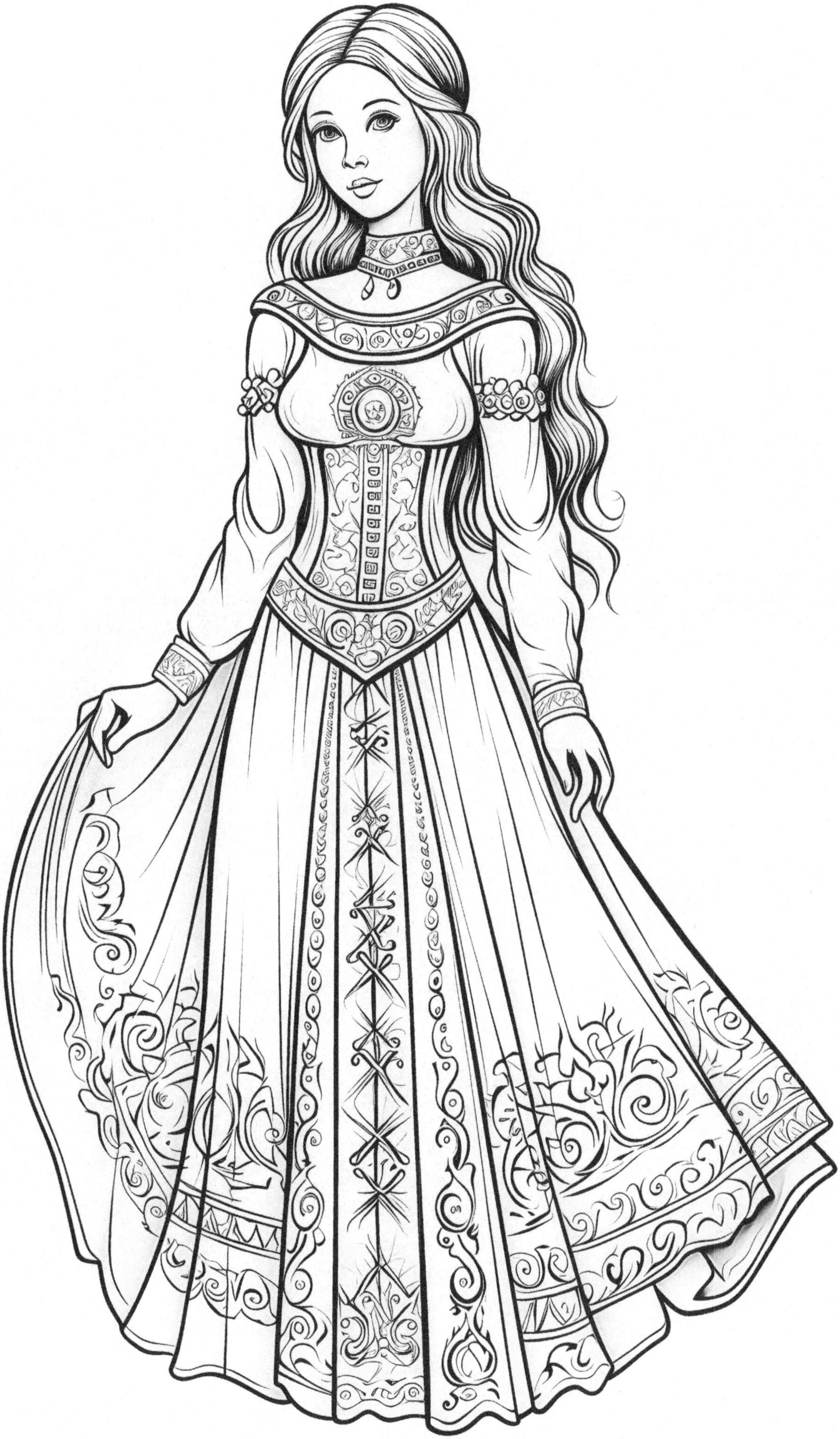

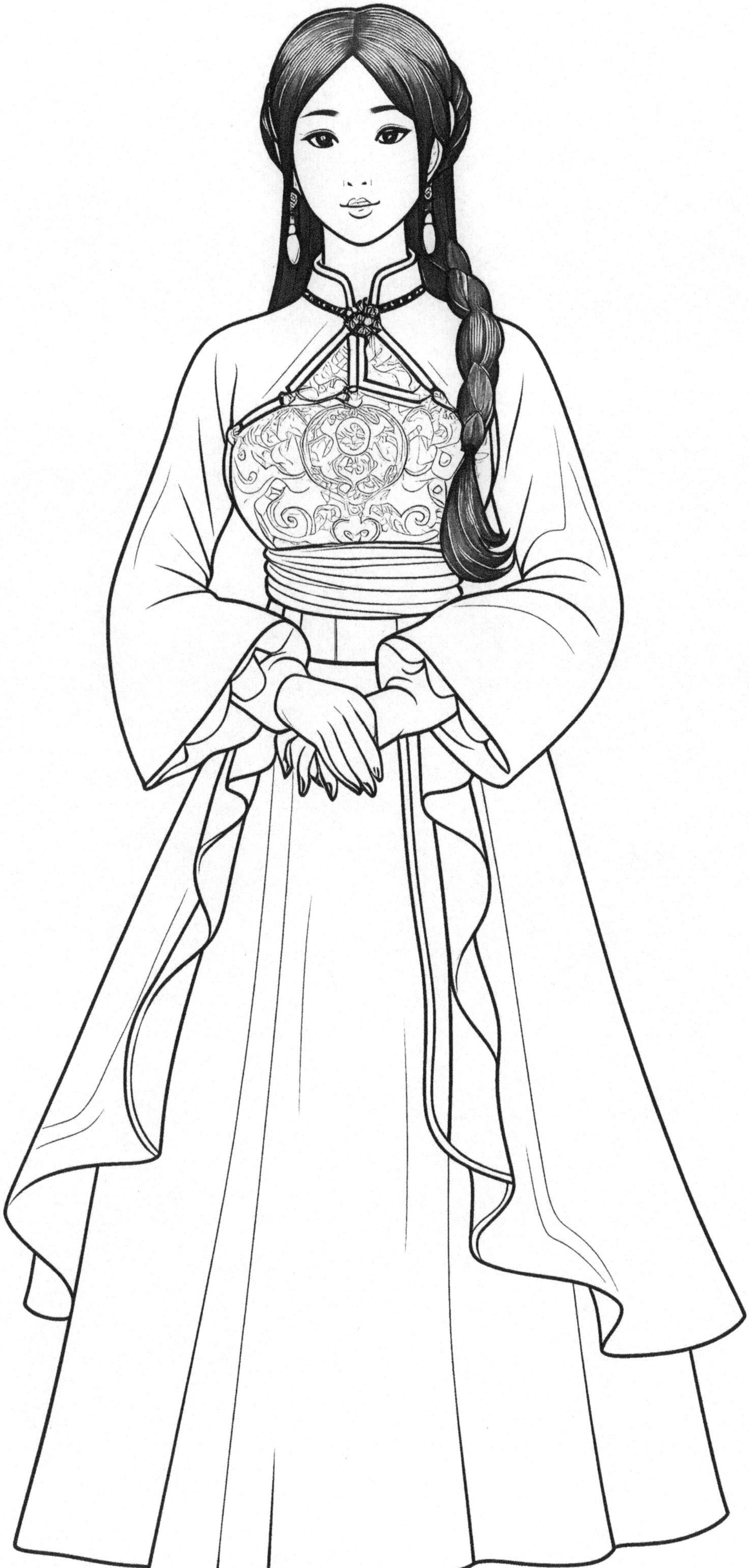

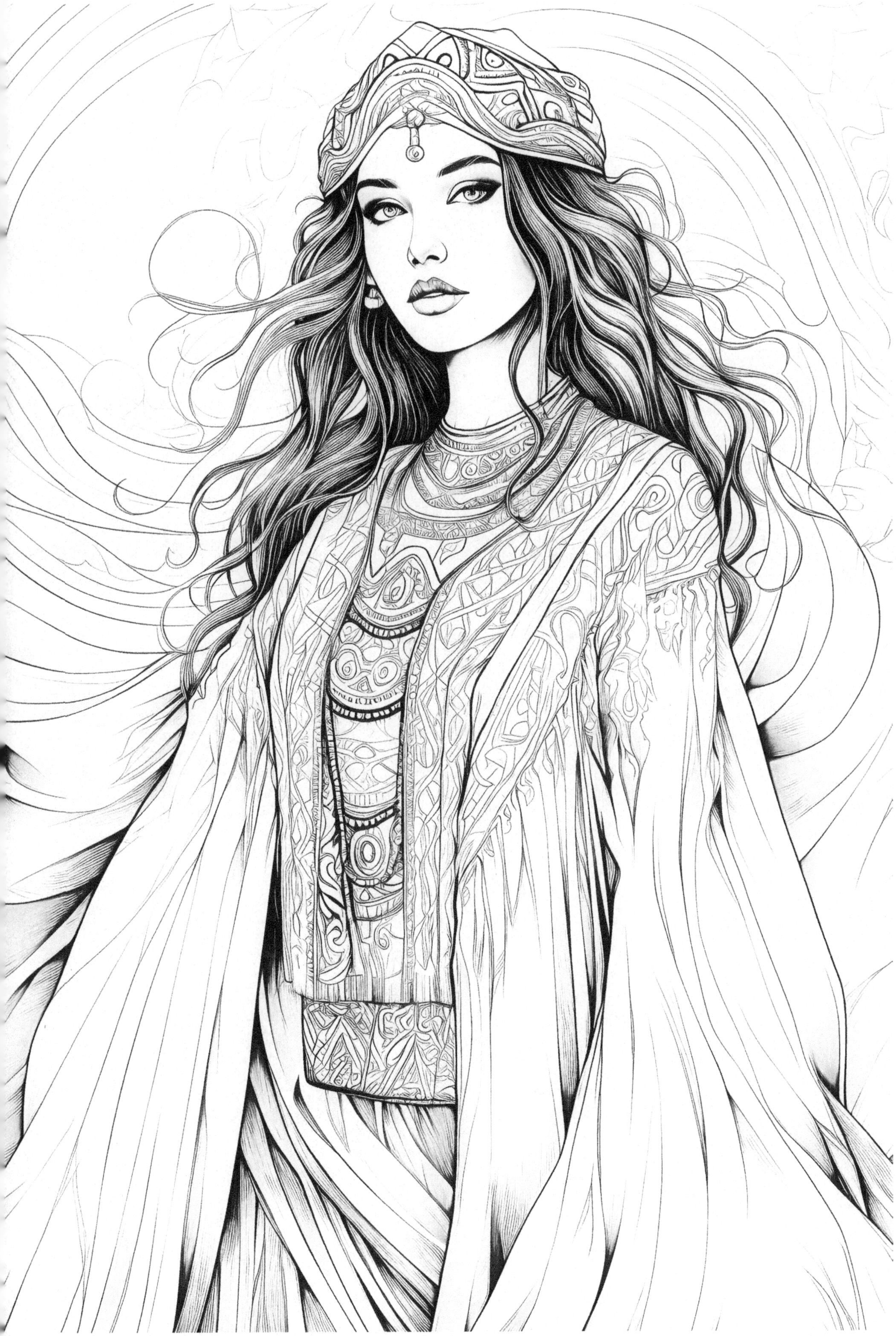

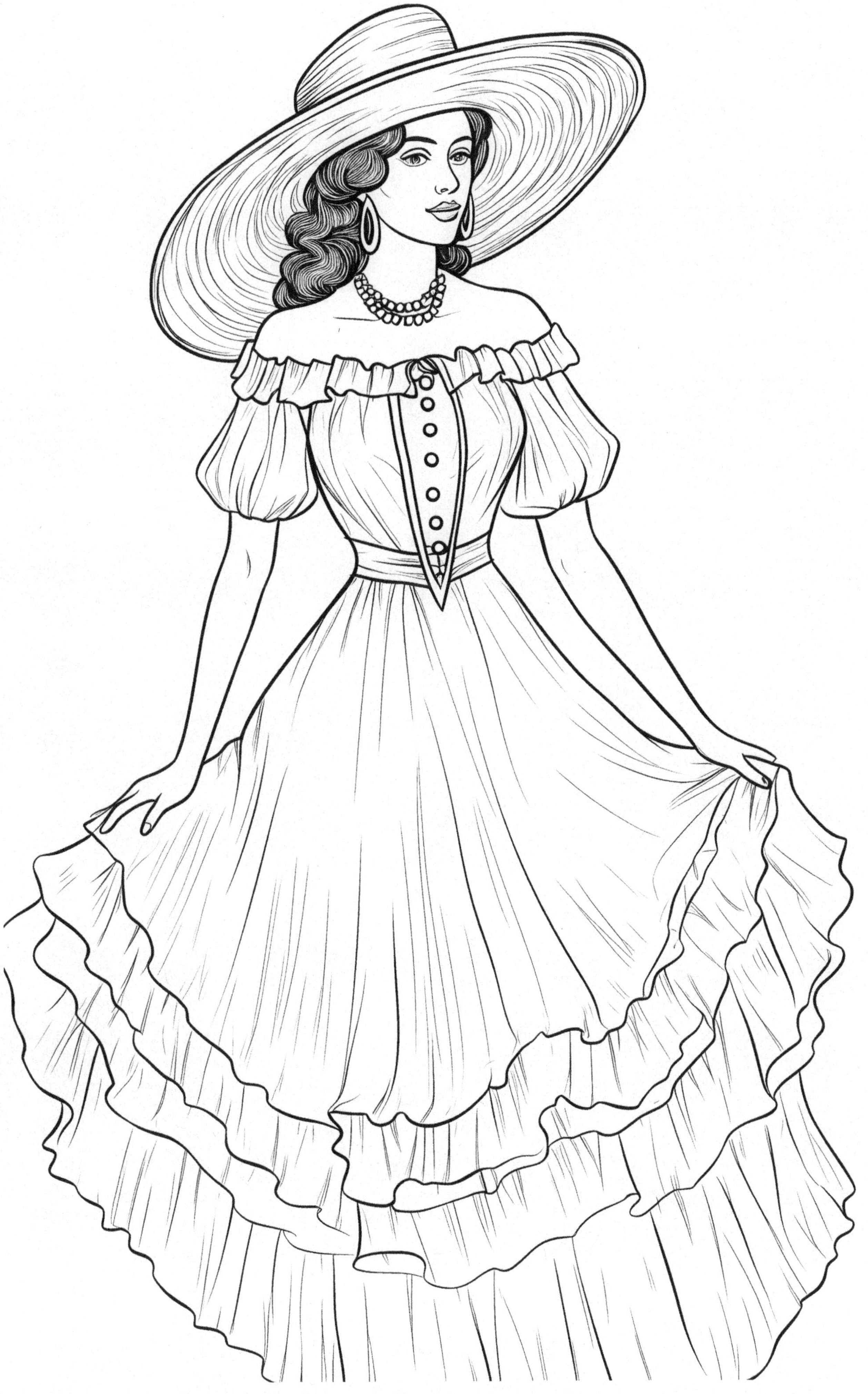

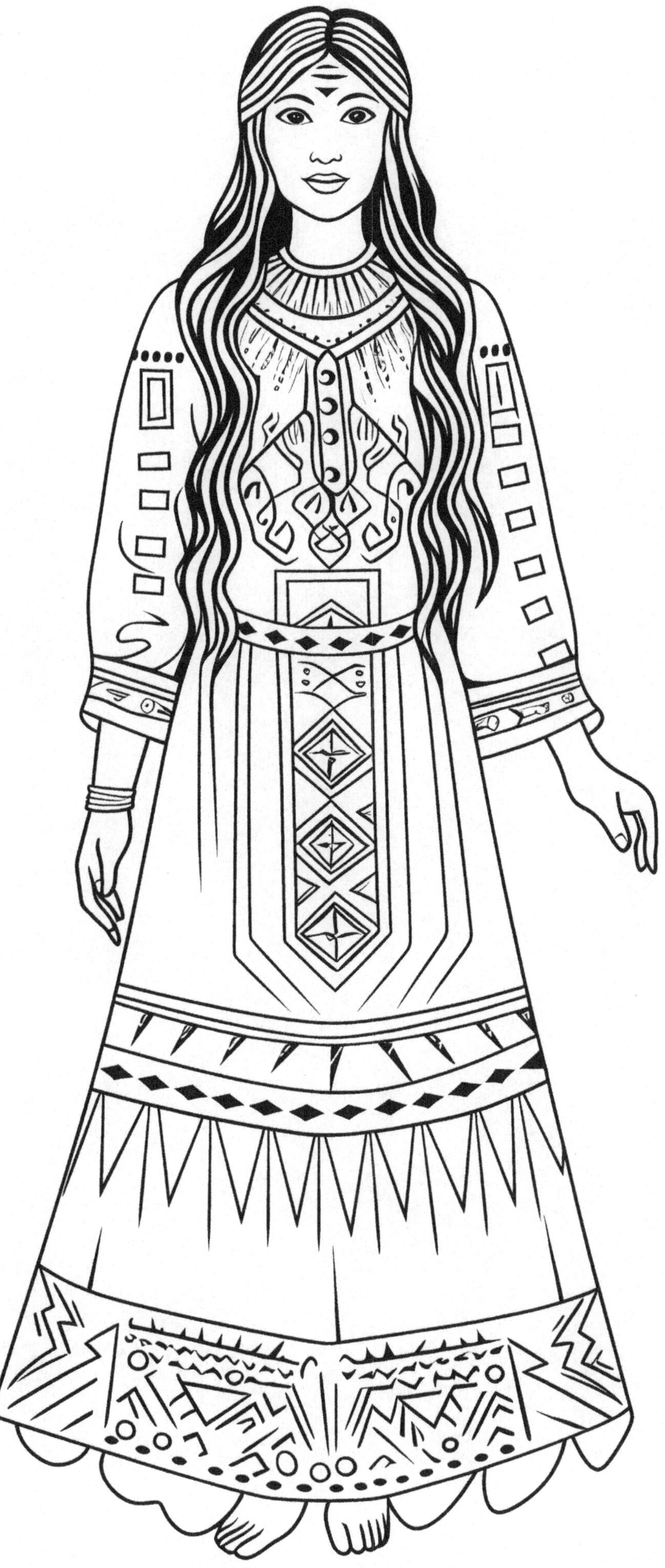

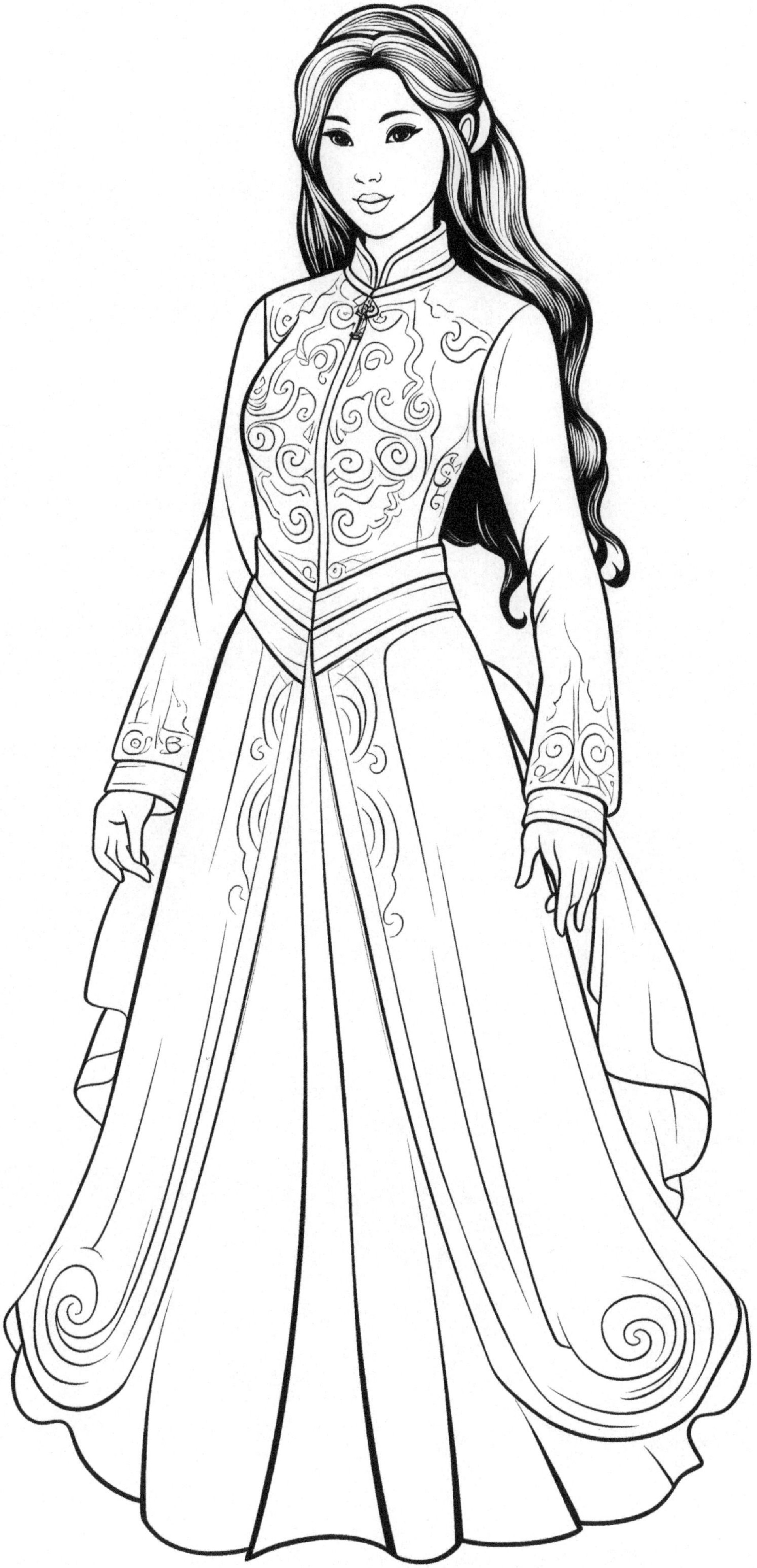

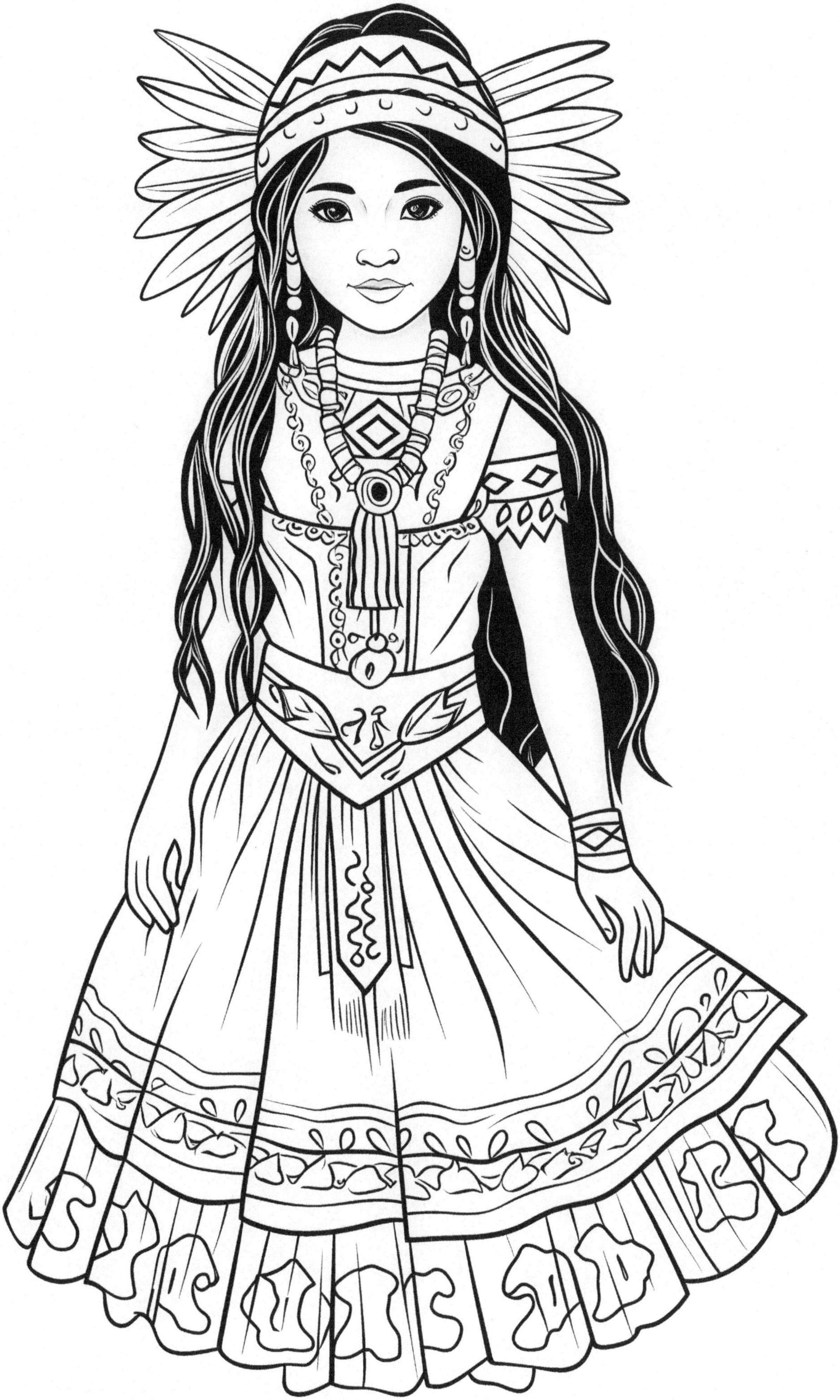

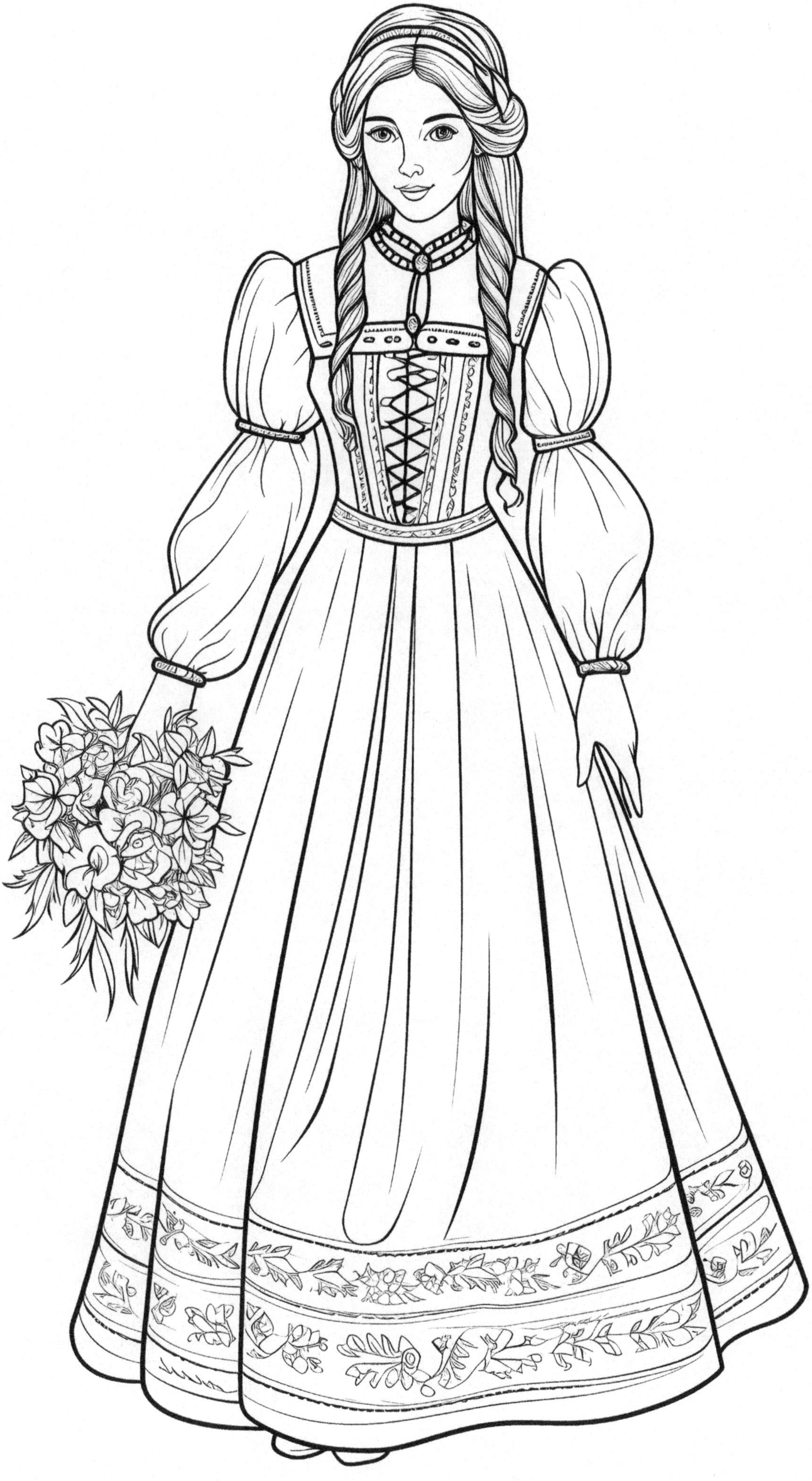

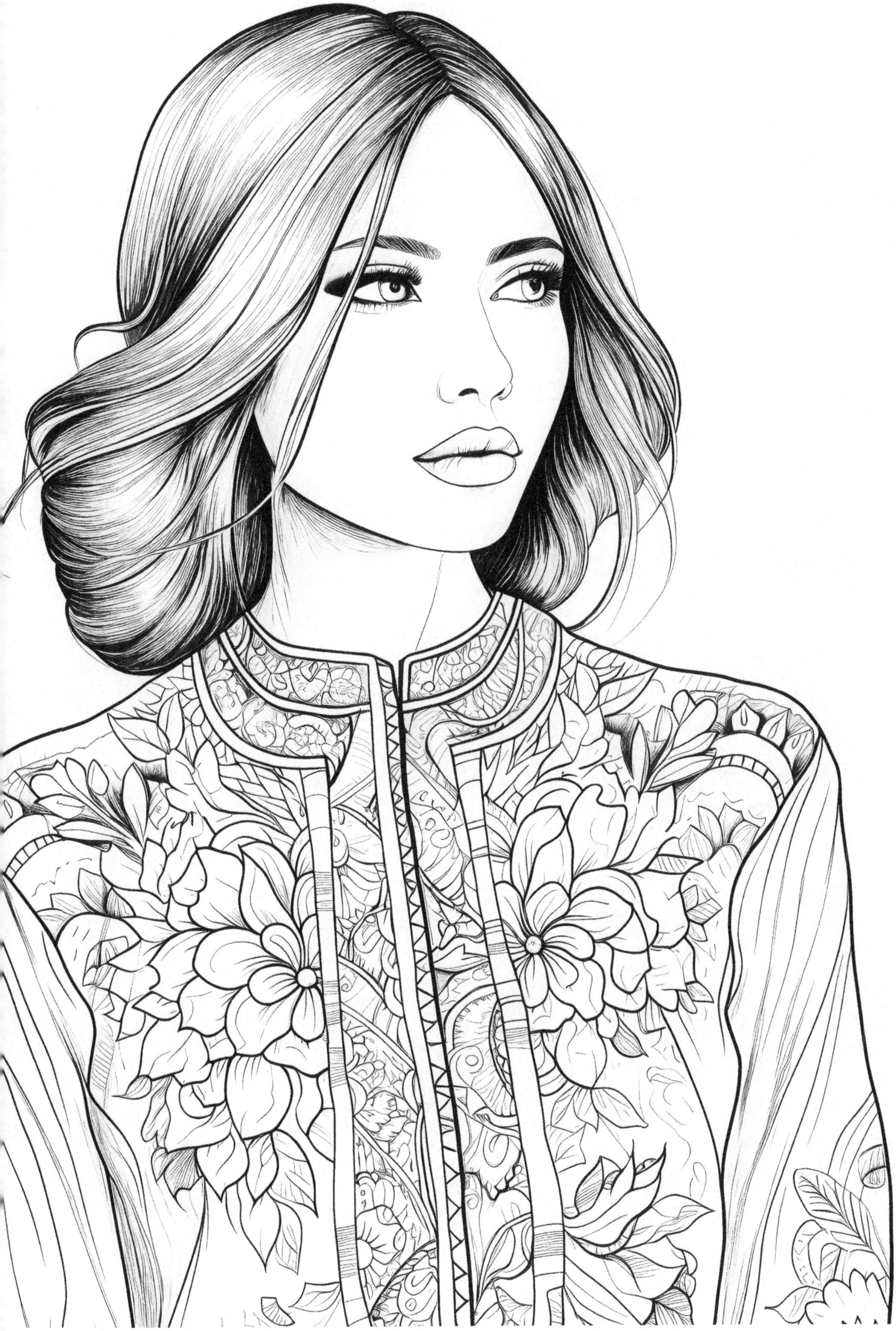

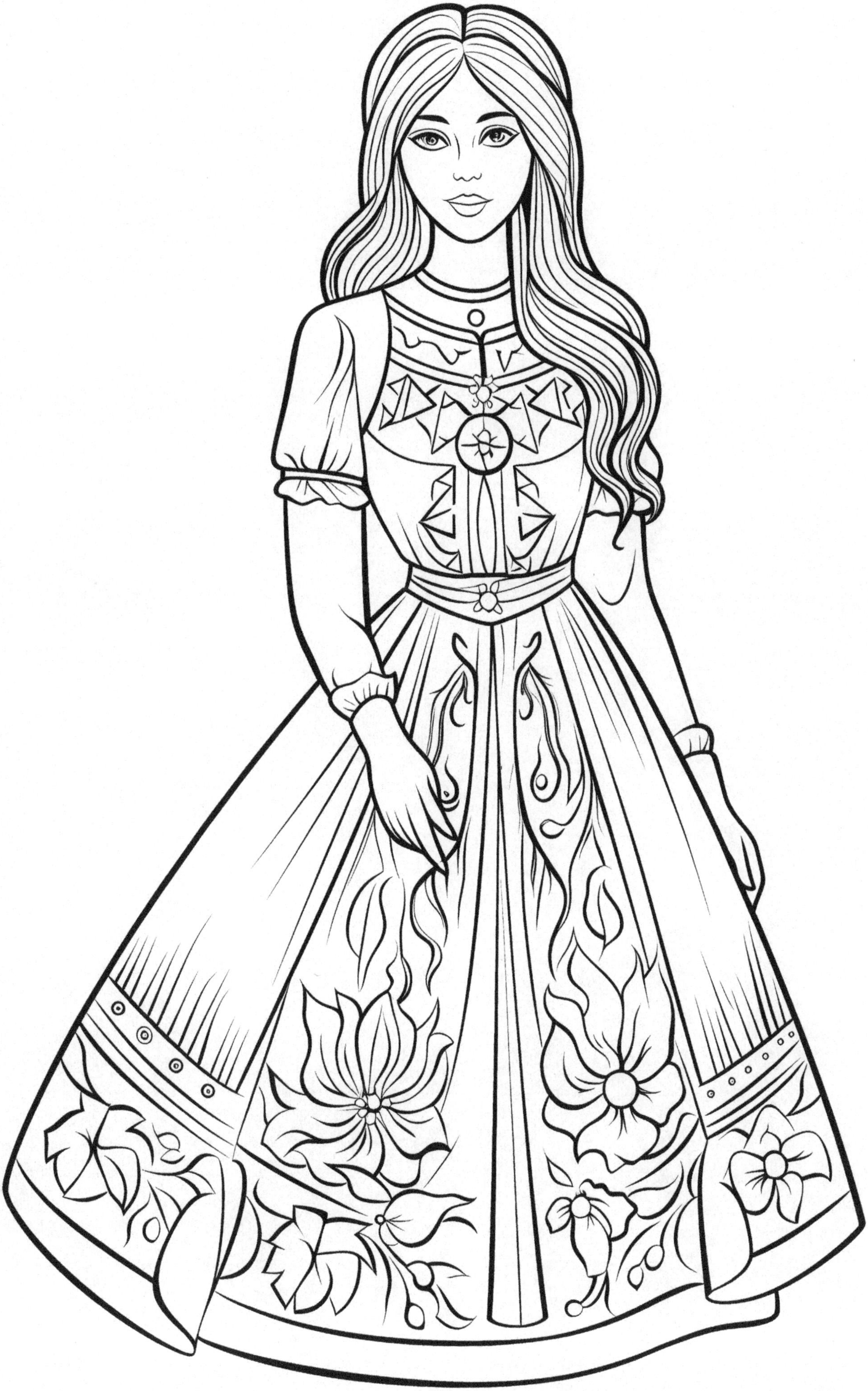

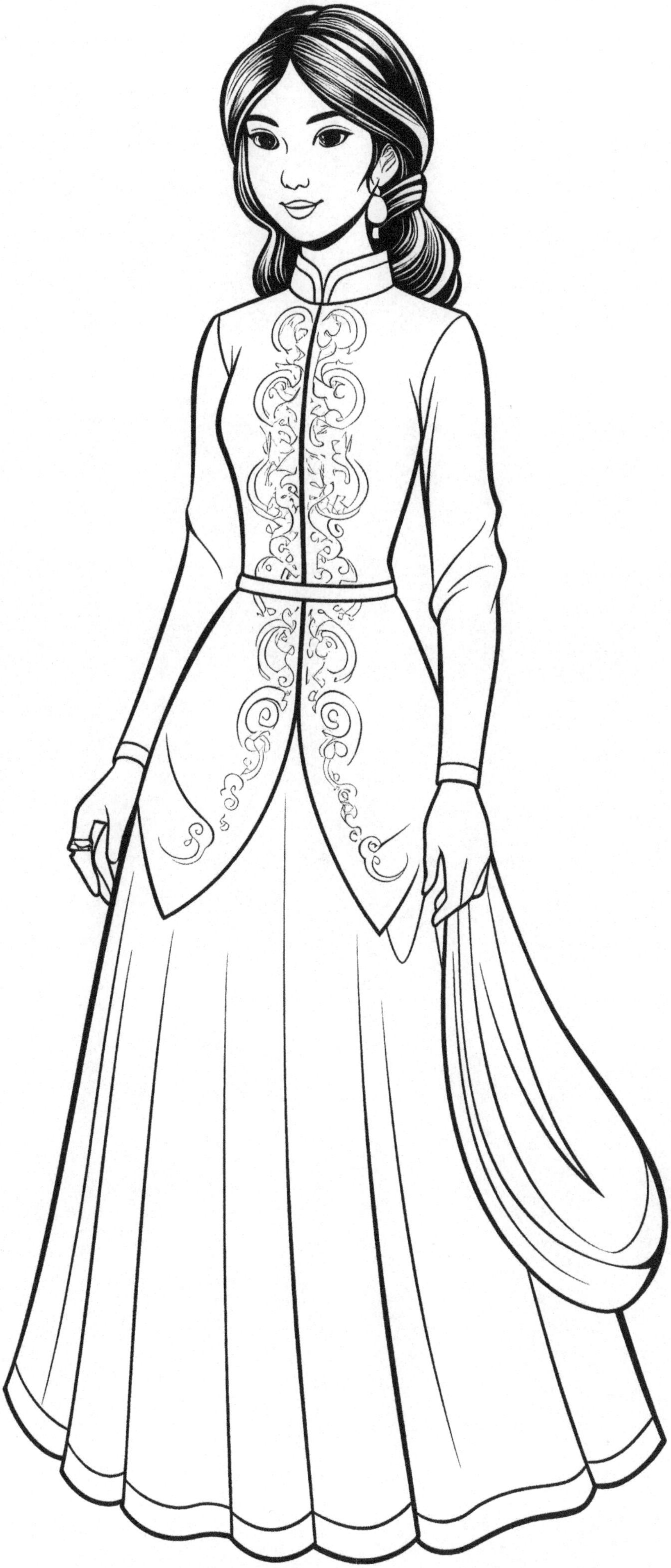

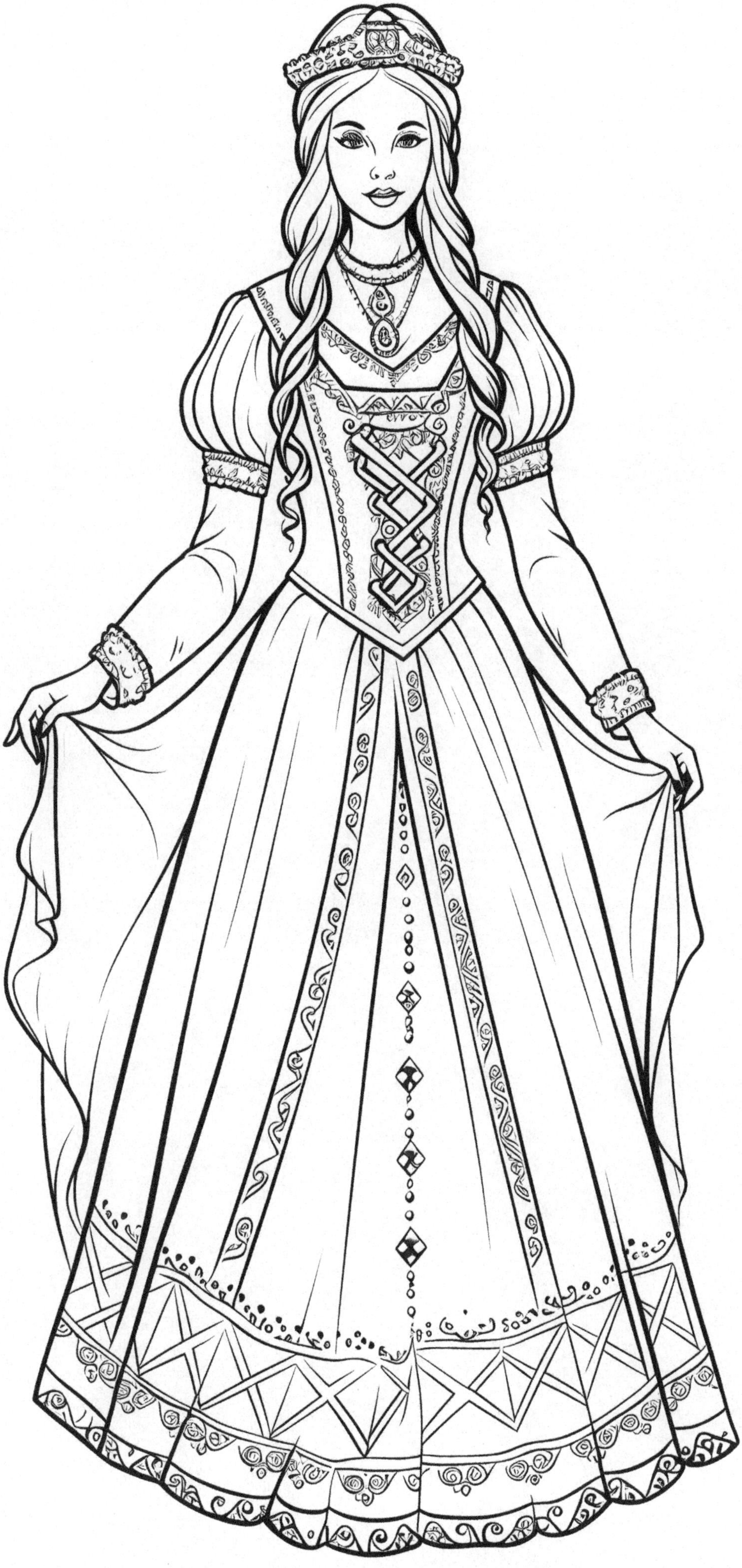

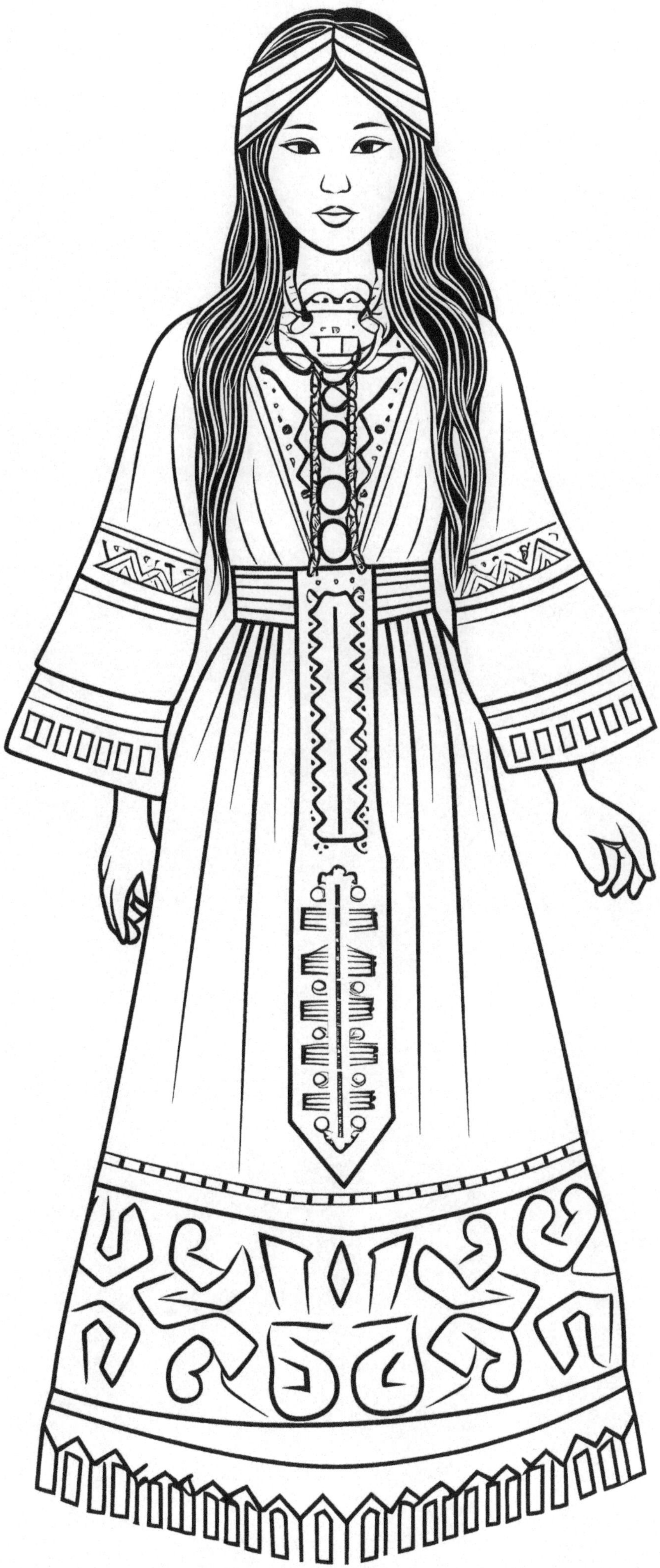

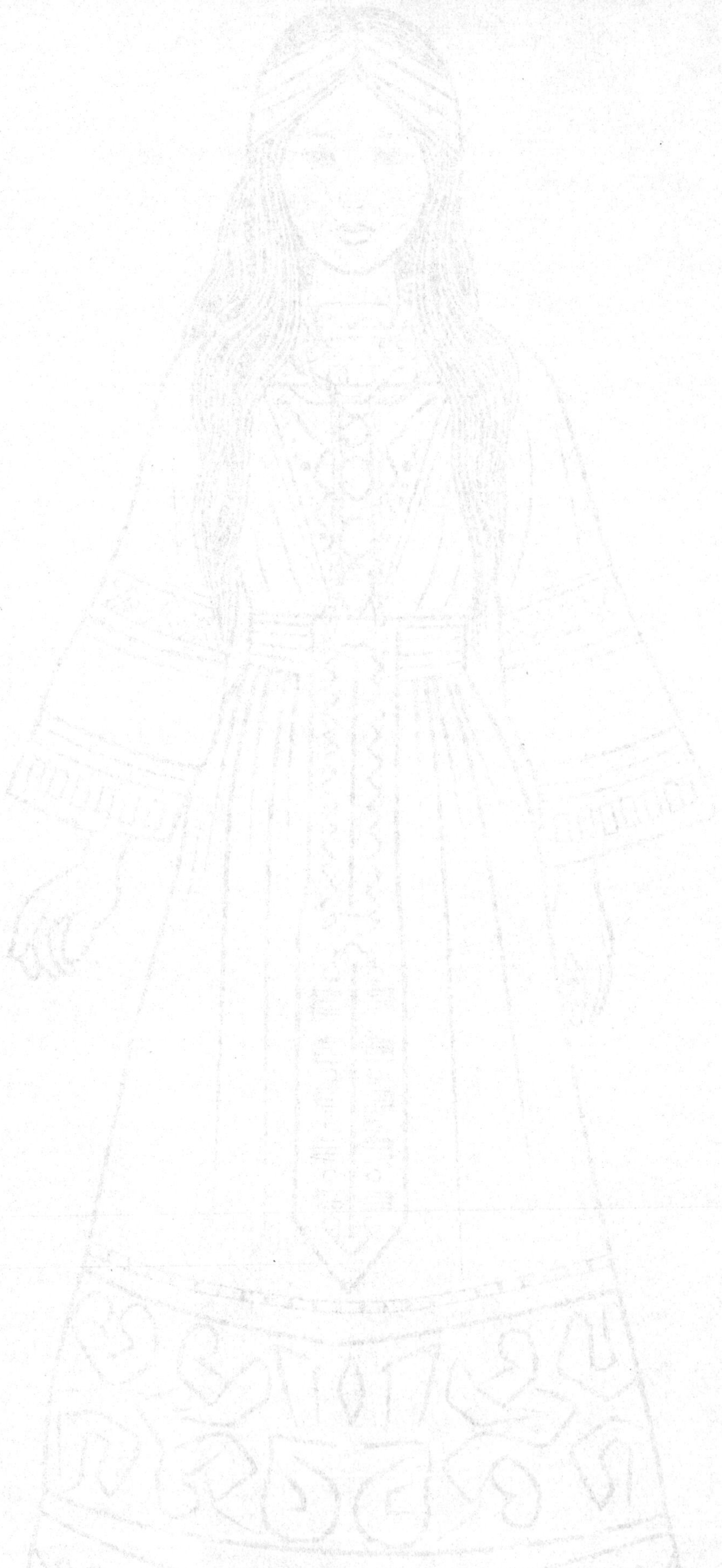

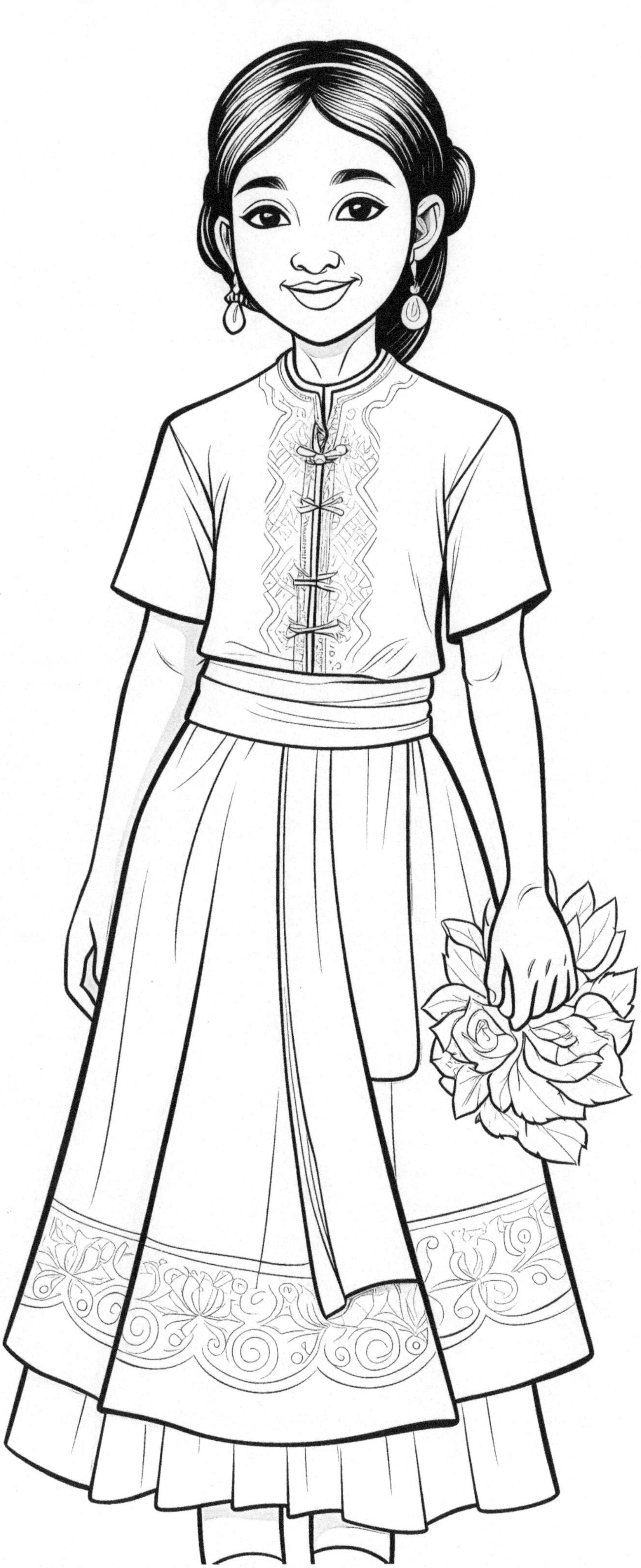

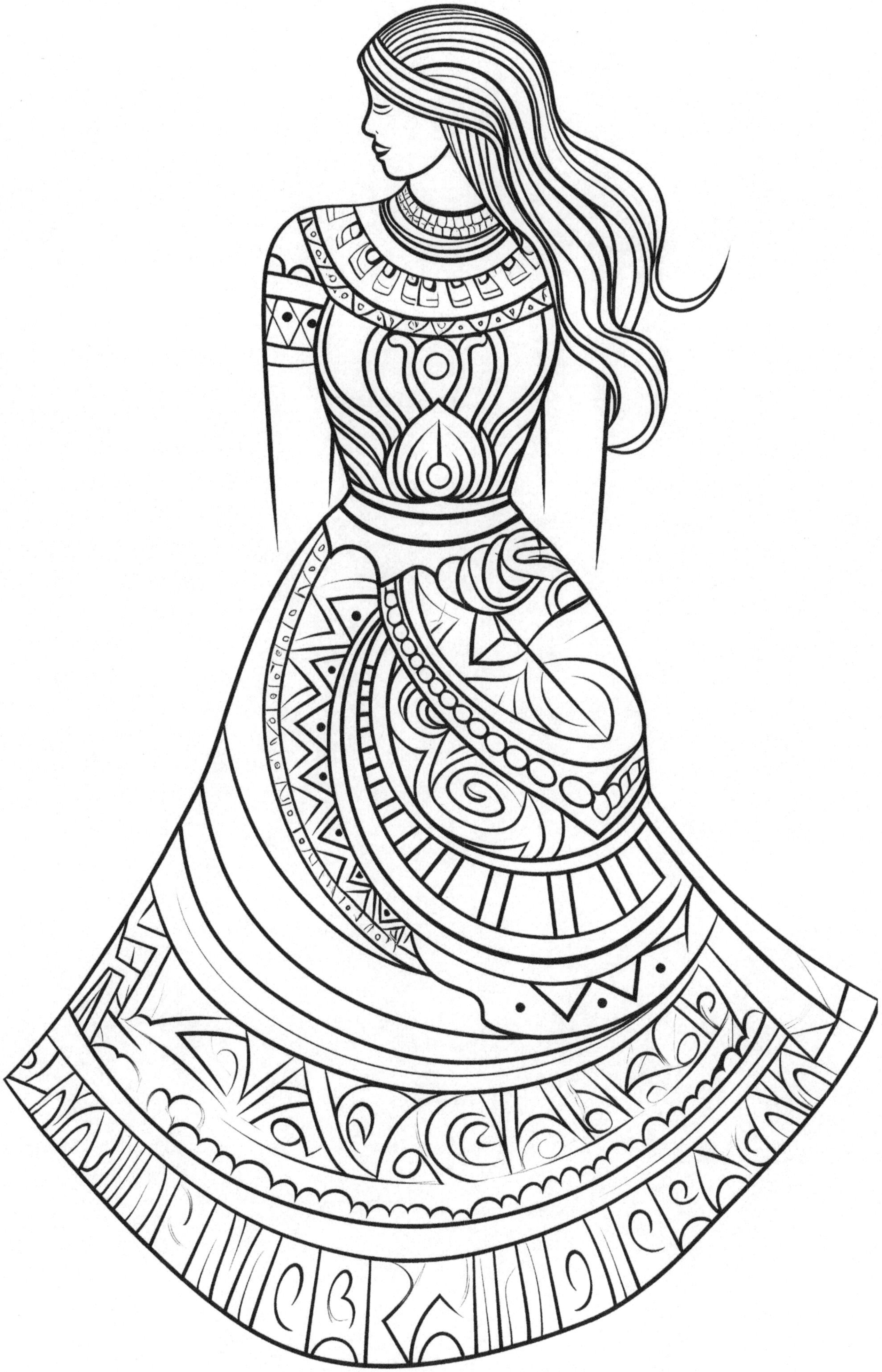

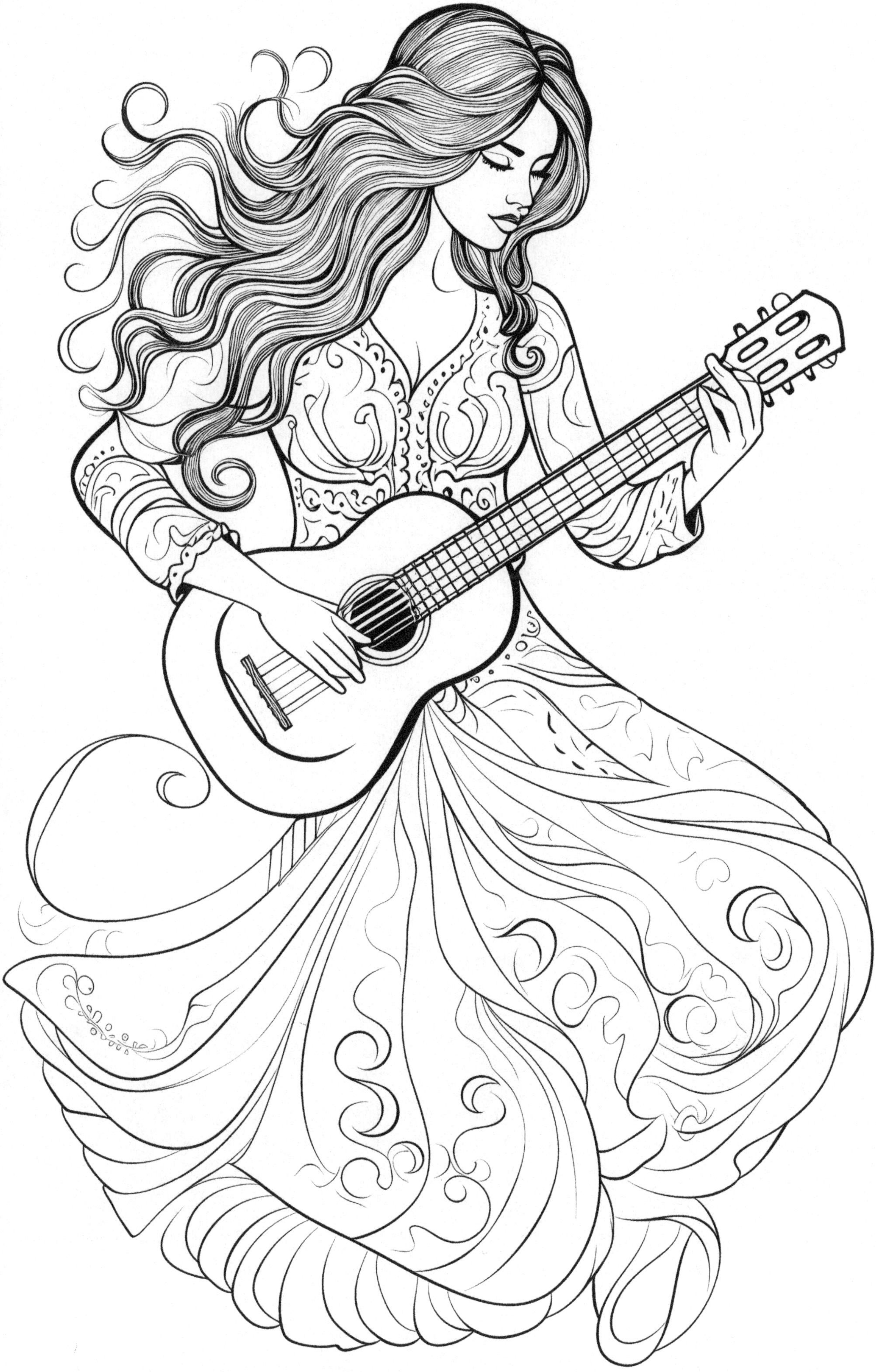

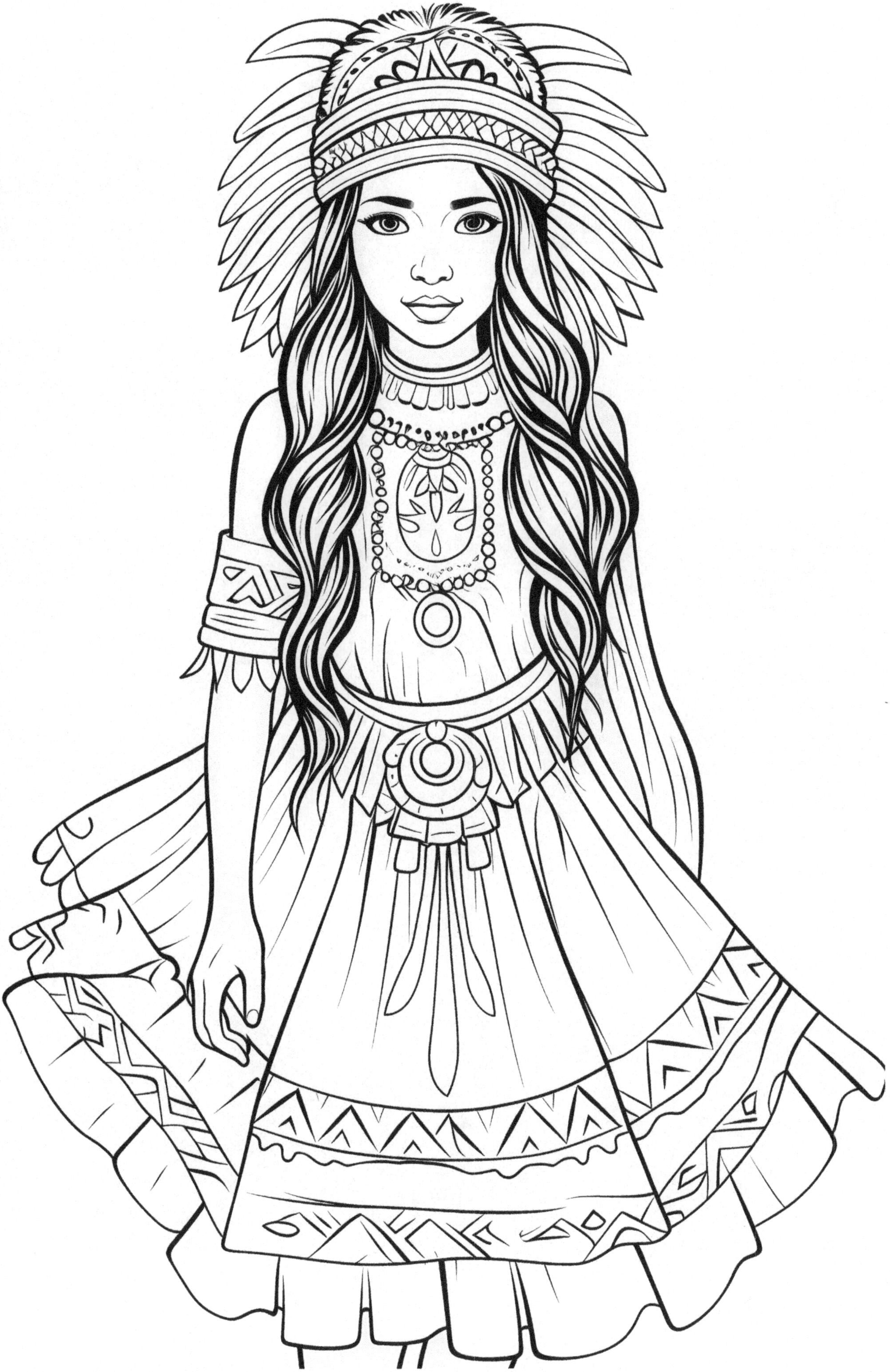

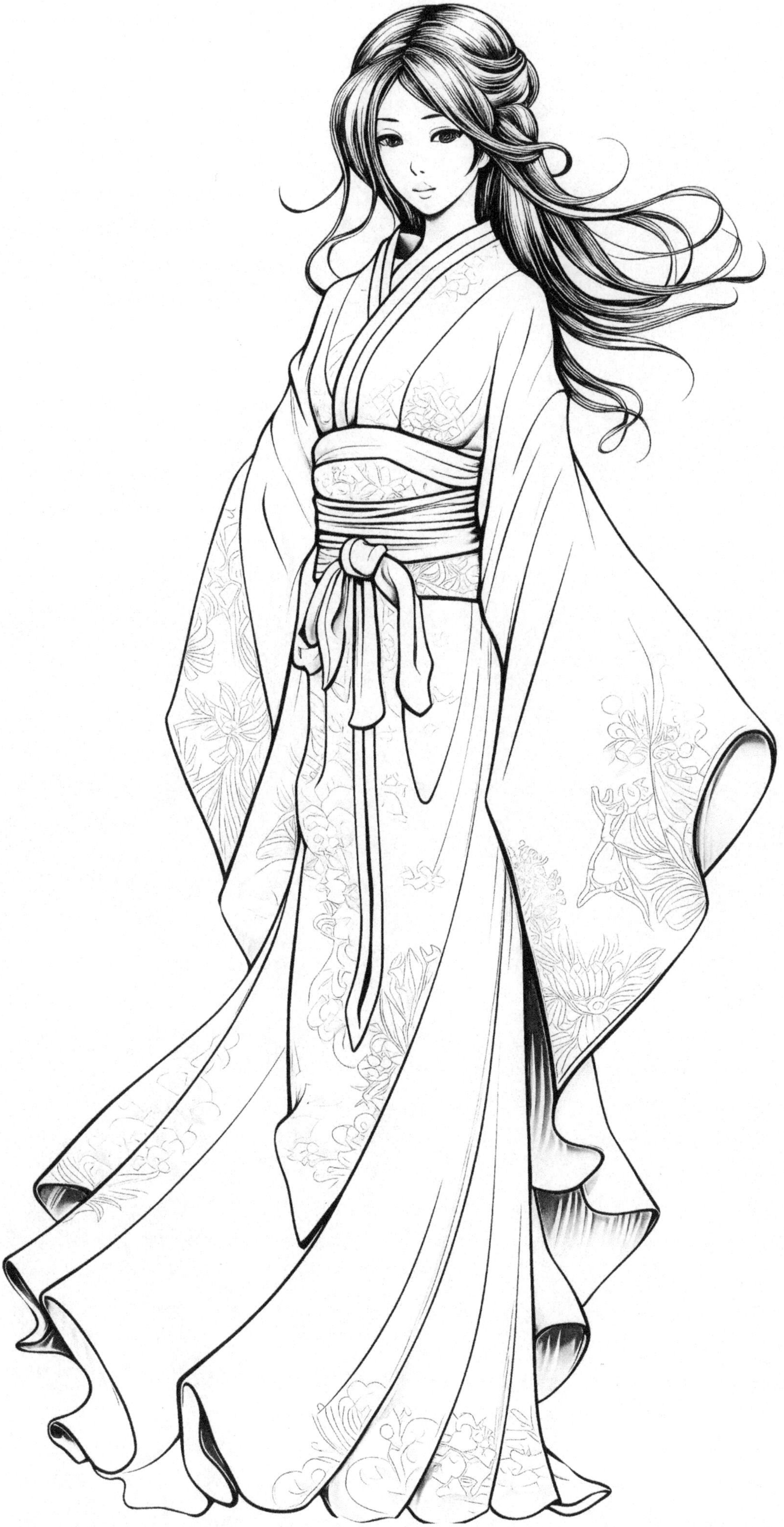

Made in the USA
Las Vegas, NV
11 December 2024

13904568R00046